Collins

Work on your
Vocabulary
Elementary **A1**

Collins

Published by Collins
An imprint of HarperCollins Publishers
Westerhill Road
Bishopbriggs
Glasgow
G64 2QT

HarperCollins Publishers
Macken House
39/40 Mayor Street Upper
Dublin 1
D01 C9W8
Ireland

First edition 2013

Reprint 11

© HarperCollins Publishers 2013

ISBN 978-0-00-749954-0

Collins® is a registered trademark of HarperCollins Publishers Limited

collins.co.uk/elt

A catalogue record for this book is available from the British Library

Typeset in India by Aptara

Printed in Great Britain by Ashford Colour Press Ltd.
Maps on page 113 © Collins Bartholomew Ltd 2013

The material in this book has been written by a team from Language Testing 123, a UK-based consultancy that specializes in English language assessment and materials. The units are by Elizabeth Walter and have been based on material from the Collins Corpus and the Collins COBUILD reference range.

www.languagetesting123.co

Contents

Introduction

Welcome to *Work on your Vocabulary – Elementary (A1)*.

Is this the right book for me?

This book, *Work on your Vocabulary – Elementary (A1)*, helps students to learn and practise English vocabulary at CEF level A1. This book is suitable for you to use if you are at CEF level A1, or just below.

So, what is CEF level A1? Well, there are six Common European Framework levels. They go up from A1 for beginners, A2, B1, B2, C1 and finally C2.

If the description below sounds like you, then this is probably the right book for you. If you think your English is higher in level than this, choose *Work on your Vocabulary – Pre-Intermediate (A2)*.

- I can understand and use common words and expressions.
- I know words for talking about everyday things, such as my daily life, my home and friends and family.
- I can have simple conversations with people.
- I need people to talk slowly and clearly to me.
- I'm sure I make lots of mistakes!

What does this book contain?

This book contains 30 units to help you learn and practise important vocabulary for this elementary (A1) level.

Each unit gives you **explanations** and **definitions** of the words and expressions for the topic area, in the **Word Finder** boxes.

There is a series of **exercises** that give you useful practice in this particular area.

The **answers** to all the exercises are at the back of the book.

At the back of the book, you'll also find a list of all the words introduced in the book (the **Index**). Each word has the unit number next to it, so you can find it easily in the main part of the book.

There are **Good to know!** boxes to help you to pay attention to important information about the words and expressions.

I'm a student: how can I use this book?

You can use this book in different ways. It depends on your needs, and the time that you have.

- If you have a teacher, he or she may give you some advice about using the book.
- If you are working alone, you may decide to study the complete book from beginning to end, starting with Unit 1 and working your way through to the end.
- You might find that it is better to choose which units you need to study first, which might not be the first units in the book. Take control of what you learn and choose the units you feel are most important for you.
- You may also decide to use the book for reference when you are not sure about a particular vocabulary topic.
- You can find what you want to learn about by looking in the **Contents** page.
- Please note that, if you do not understand something in one unit, you may need to study a unit earlier in the book for more explanation.

Study tips

1 Read the aim and introduction to the unit carefully.

2 Read the explanation. Sometimes, there is a short text or dialogue; sometimes there are tables of information; sometimes there are examples with notes. These are to help you understand the most important information about this area of vocabulary.

3 Don't read the explanation too quickly: spend time trying to understand it as well as you can. If you don't understand, read it again more slowly.

4 Do the exercises. Don't do them too quickly: think carefully about the answers. If you don't feel sure, look at the explanation and Word Finder box again. Write your answers in pencil, or, even better, on a separate piece of paper. (This means that you can do the exercises again later.)

5 Check your answers to the exercises in the back of the book.

6 If you get every answer correct, congratulations! Don't worry if you make some mistakes. Studying your mistakes is an important part of learning.

7 Look carefully at each mistake: can you now see why the correct answer is what it is?

8 Read the explanation and definitions again to help you understand.

9 Finally, if the unit includes a **Good to know!** box, then try really hard to remember what it says. It contains a special piece of information about the words and expressions.

10 Always return: come back and do the unit's exercises again a few days later. This helps you to keep the information in your head for longer.

I want to improve my vocabulary

Good! Only using one book won't be enough to really make your vocabulary improve. The most important thing is you!

Buy a good dictionary for your level. You could try the *Collins COBUILD Intermediate Learner's Dictionary* or the *Collins COBUILD Primary Learner's Dictionary*. *Collins Easy Learning English Vocabulary* might also be a useful book to have.

Of course, you need to have a notebook, paper or electronic. Try these six techniques for getting the best from it.

- *Make it personal:* When you're learning a new word or expression, try to write some examples about yourself or people or places you know. It's easier to remember sentences about your life than someone else's! For example, *I have one older brother and two younger sisters.*

- *Look out:* Everything you read or hear in English may contain some examples of the new vocabulary you're learning. Try to notice these examples. Also, try to write down some of these examples, so that you can learn them.

- *Think aloud:* Practise saying the new words aloud. It helps you to remember them better. Also, pronunciation is very important; people need to understand you!

- *Everywhere you go:* Take your notebook with you. Use spare moments, such as when you're waiting for a friend to arrive. Read through your notes. Try to repeat things from memory. A few minutes here and there add up to a useful learning system.

- *Take it further:* Don't just learn the examples in the book. Keep making your own examples, and learning those.

- *Don't stop:* It's really important to keep learning. If you don't keep practising, you won't remember for very long. Practise the new vocabulary today, tomorrow, the next day, a week later and a month later.

I'm a teacher: how can I use this book with my classes?

The contents included have been very carefully selected by experts from Language Testing 123, using the Common European Framework for Reference, English Profile, the British Council Core Inventory, the Collins Corpus and the Collins COBUILD dictionaries range. As such, it represents a useful body of knowledge for students to acquire at this level. The language used is designed to be of effective general relevance and interest to any learner aged 14+.

The units use a range of exercise types to engage with students and to usefully practise what they have learnt from the explanation pages on the left. There are enough exercises for each unit that it is not necessary for students to do all the exercises at one sitting. Rather, you may wish to return in later sessions to complete the remaining exercises.

The book will be a valuable self-study resource for students studying on their own. You can also integrate into the teaching that you provide for your students.

The explanations and exercises, while designed for self-study, can be easily adapted by you to provide useful interactive work for your students in class.

You will probably use the units in the book to extend, back up or consolidate language work you are doing in class. This means you will probably make a careful choice about which unit to do at a particular time.

You may also find that you recommend certain units to students who are experiencing particular difficulty with specific language areas. Alternatively, you may use various units in the book as an aid to revision.

Lesson plan

1 Read the aim and introduction to the unit carefully: is it what you want your students to focus on? Make sure the students understand it.

2 Go through the explanation with your students. You may read this aloud to them, or ask them to read it silently to themselves. With a confident class, you could ask them to read some of it aloud.

3 If there is a dialogue, you could ask students to perform it. If there is a text, you could extend it in some way that makes it particularly relevant to your students. Certainly, you should provide a pronunciation model of focus language.

4 Take time over the explanation page, and check students' understanding. Use concept-checking questions.

5 Perhaps do the first exercise together with the class. Don't do it too quickly: encourage students to think carefully about the answers. If they don't feel sure, look together at the explanation again.

6 Now get students to do the other exercises. They can work alone, or perhaps in pairs, discussing the answers. This will involve useful speaking practice and also more careful consideration of the information. Tell students to write their answers in pencil, or, even better, on a separate piece of paper. (This means that they can do the exercises again later.)

7 Check their answers to the exercises in the back of the book. Discuss the questions and problems they have.

8   If the unit includes a **Good to know!** box, then tell students to try really hard to remember what it says. It contains a special piece of information about the words and expressions.

9   Depending on your class and the time available, there are different ways you could extend the learning. If one of the exercises is in the form of an email, you could ask your students to write a reply to it. If the exercises are using spoken language, then you can ask students to practise these as bits of conversation. They can re-write the exercises with sentences that are about themselves and each other. Maybe pairs of students can write an exercise of their own together and these can be distributed around the class. Maybe they can write little stories or dialogues including the focus language and perform these to the class.

10 Discuss with the class what notes they should make about the language in the unit. Encourage them to make effective notes, perhaps demonstrating this on the board for them, and/or sharing different ideas from the class.

11 Always return: come back and repeat at least some of the unit's exercises again a few days later. This helps your students to keep the information in their heads for longer.

Guide to word classes

All the words in **Word Finder** boxes have a word class. The table below gives you more information about each of these word classes.

Word class	Description
ADJECTIVE	An adjective is a word that is used for telling you more about a person or thing. You use adjectives to talk about appearance, colour, size, or other qualities, e.g. *He has got **short** hair.*
ADVERB	An adverb is a word that gives more information about when, how, or where something happens, e.g. *She went **inside**.*
CONJUNCTION	A conjunction is a word such as *and*, *but*, *if*, and *since*. Conjunctions are used for linking two words or two parts of a sentence together, e.g. *I'm tired **and** hungry.*
NOUN	A noun is a word that refers to a person, a thing, or a quality, e.g. *I live in the **city**.*
PHRASAL VERB	A phrasal verb consists of a verb and one or more particles, e.g. *When I go outside, I **put on** a warm coat.*
PHRASE	Phrases are groups of words that are used together and that have a meaning of their own, e.g. *I **would like** to get a new job.*
PLURAL NOUN	A plural noun is always plural, and it is used with plural verbs, e.g. *My **clothes** are in my suitcase.*
PREPOSITION	A preposition is a word such as **below**, **by**, **with**, or **from** that is always followed by a noun group or the **-ing** form of a verb. Prepositions are usually used to say where things are, e.g. *You can park **outside** the house.*
PRONOUN	A pronoun is a word that you use instead of a noun, when you do not need or want to name someone or something directly, e.g. ***He** lives in London; you need to try several different ways of doing **it**.*
VERB	A verb is a word that is used for saying what someone or something does, or what happens to them, or to give information about them, e.g. *Can I **pay** by credit card?*

1

Talking about yourself

Where I live

My **name** is Louisa. I **live** in the **countryside** with my **family**.

My **name** is Thomas. I **live** in the **city**. I am a **student**. I go to **university**.

Giving information

First Name: |J|u|l|i|a|_|_|_|_|_|_|_|_|_|_|_|_|_|_|_|_|_|_|_|_|_|_|_|_|_|_|_|

Family Name: |W|i|l|s|o|n|_|_|_|_|_|_|_|_|_|_|_|_|_|_|_|_|_|_|_|_|_|_|_|_|_|

Address:

Number: |_|_|3|6|_| Street: |M|i|l|l| |R|o|a|d|_|_|_|_|_|_|_|_|_|_|_|_|_|

Town/City: |C|a|m|b|r|i|d|g|e|_|_|_|_|_|_|_|_|_|_|_|_|_|_|_|_|_|

Age: _23_____ Nationality: _British___

Good to know!

It is important to use the right prepositions:
I was born <u>in</u> 1999.
I live <u>in</u> the city.
Dad is <u>at</u> work.
I go <u>to</u> school/college/university.
I study English <u>at</u> school/college/university.

Words for talking about yourself

address	NOUN Your **address** is the number of the building, the name of the street, and the town or city where you live or work.
age	NOUN Your **age** is the number of years that you have lived.
be ... years old	PHRASE If someone **is twelve years old**, they have lived for twelve years.
born	VERB When a baby is **born**, it comes out of its mother's body and begins life.
city	NOUN A **city** is a large town.
college	NOUN **College** is a place where students study after they leave school.
countryside	NOUN The **countryside** is land that is away from cities and towns.
family	NOUN A **family** is a group of people who are related to each other, usually parents and their children.
family name	NOUN Your **family name** is the part of your name that all the people in your family have.
first name	NOUN Your **first name** is the name that comes before your family name.
job	NOUN A **job** is the work that someone does to earn money.
live	VERB If you **live** somewhere, you have your home in that place.
name	NOUN A person's **name** is the word or words that you use to talk to them, or to talk about them.
nationality	NOUN If you have the **nationality** of a particular country, you are a legal citizen of that country.
school	NOUN A **school** is a place where people go to learn.
street	NOUN A **street** is a road in a city or a town.
student	NOUN A **student** is a person who is studying at a school, college, or university.
study	1 VERB If you **study**, you spend time learning about a particular subject. 2 NOUN **Study** is the activity of studying.
university	NOUN A **university** is a place where you can study after school.
work	VERB People who **work** have a job and earn money for it.

Exercise 1

Put the correct word in each gap, as shown.

| college | lives | first | years | student | age | family |

My best friend

My best friend's ¹_____*first*_____ name is Jane and her ²_____ name is Johnson.
She ³_____ in Manchester with her mother and father. She is 17 ⁴_____
old. She likes dancing. Jane is a ⁵_____ and is studying marketing at
⁶_____.

Exercise 2

Match the sentence halves, as shown.

1 I was born
2 I live in
3 My address
4 I am 19
5 I have
6 I study at a

a big city.
b French nationality.
c in 1993.
d years old.
e is 21 Hope Street.
f university.

Exercise 3

Choose the correct word or words, as shown.

1 I live in a small **city** / **countryside** / **address**.
2 My first name is **Peter / Mr Johnson / student**.
3 I live with my **family / school / nationality**.
4 I am studying at school, so I don't have a **name / job / student**.
5 I am 18 **age / born / years old**.

Exercise 4

Put the correct word in each gap, as shown.

| university | family | born | study | job | name | work |

Dear penfriend,

Hi, my ¹_____ *name* _____ is Ronald Harrison and I ²_____ in a restaurant.
I live with my ³_____ in a big house near the city. Next year, I want to go to
⁴_____. I want to ⁵_____ to be a doctor. I like reading and watching TV.
I was ⁶_____ in 1995.

Write soon!
Ronald

Exercise 5

Find the wrong or extra word in each sentence, as shown.

1 What is ✗ your name?
2 Where address do you live?
3 How age old are you?
4 What nationality country have you got?
5 Are you a student school?
6 What work is your job?

Family

Look at the family tree:

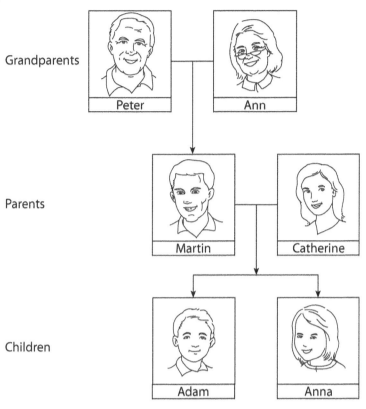

Grandparents — Peter, Ann

Parents — Martin, Catherine

Children — Adam, Anna

Peter is Adam and Anna's **grandfather**.
Ann is Adam and Anna's **grandmother**.
Martin is Adam and Anna's **father**.
Catherine is Adam and Anna's **mother**.
Adam is Martin and Catherine's **son**.
Anna is Martin and Catherine's **daughter**.
Adam is Anna's **brother**.
Anna is Adam's **sister**.

Good to know!

Mother and *father* are slightly formal words. When you talk with friends or family about your own parents, it is usual to say *mum* and *dad*.

Words for talking about family

be ... years old	PHRASE The number of **years old** that someone is means the number of years they have lived.
boy	NOUN A **boy** is a male child.
brother	NOUN A **brother** is a boy or a man who has the same parents as you.
child	NOUN A **child** is a young boy or girl.
children	NOUN **Children** is the plural of child.
dad	NOUN Your **dad** is your father.
daughter	NOUN Someone's **daughter** is their female child.
family	NOUN A **family** is a group of people who are related to each other, usually parents and their children.
family name	NOUN Your **family name** is the part of your name that all the people in your family have.
father	NOUN Your **father** is your male parent.
girl	NOUN A **girl** is a female child.
grandad	NOUN **Grandad** is an informal name for grandfather.
grandfather	NOUN Your **grandfather** is the father of your father or mother.
grandma	NOUN **Grandma** is an informal name for a grandmother.
grandmother	NOUN Your **grandmother** is the mother of your father or mother.
man	NOUN A **man** is an adult male human.
mother	NOUN Your **mother** is your female parent.
mum	NOUN **Mum** is an informal name for your mother.
old	ADJECTIVE Someone who is **old** has lived for many years and is not young.
sister	NOUN Your **sister** is a girl or woman who has the same parents as you.
son	NOUN Someone's **son** is their male child.
young	ADJECTIVE A **young** person, animal, or plant has not lived for very long.

Exercise 1

Find the words or phrases that do not belong, as shown.

1 **Family members**	brother	boy	sister
2 **Ages**	old	young	family
3 **Women**	grandfather	sister	daughter
4 **Family members**	grandmother	father	young
5 **People**	old	man	girl
6 **Men**	brother	son	daughter
7 **Family members**	mother	family name	grandma
8 **What you can call certain people**	old	dad	mum

Exercise 2

Put the correct word or words in each gap.

family | children | mum | years old | young | brother

Hi Rosella,

My name is Maggie and I'm 14 ¹_____. I have a ²_____ called Oliver.
He's very ³_____ – only eight. We live with our ⁴_____ and dad. When I
get married, I want to have lots of ⁵_____, because I think a big ⁶_____
has fun. Please tell me about your family!

Maggie

Exercise 3

Which sentences are correct?

1 Your father's mother is your grandma.   ☑
2 Your mum is the father of your brother or sister.   ❑
3 Every boy and girl is someone's son.   ❑
4 Your sister, mother and grandmother are all part of your family.   ❑
5 Your dad is the daughter of your grandmother and grandfather. ❑
6 Your mother and father's sons are your brothers.   ❑

Exercise 4

Find the wrong or extra word in each sentence.

1 James is the six years old and he is a very happy child.
2 He has five brothers and sisters, so he comes from quite a big family name.
3 There are three brother boys and two girls.
4 Sarah, one of James's sisters girls, is married and has two children.
5 How much old was Sarah when James was born?
6 Sarah's old daughter is called Sue.

Exercise 5

Are the highlighted words correct or incorrect in the sentences?

1 William Shakespeare's **family name** ☒ was William.
2 Shakespeare was very **young** ❑ when he got married – only 19.
3 He married Anne Hathaway and they had three **children** ❑: Susanna, Hamnet and Judith.
4 Their son, Hamnet, was the only **mother** ❑ in the family.
5 Susanna and Judith were William's two **dads** ❑.
6 William was the **grandma** ❑ of Elizabeth, Susanna's daughter.

House and home

Things in your house

There are four **chairs** around the **table**.

The **bed** is in front of the **window**.

The **toilet** is next to the **shower**.

The **key** opens the **door**.

Describing your house

I live in a small **house** near the river. It has a **living room** and two **bedrooms**. It doesn't have a **dining room** but I have a **table** and two **chairs** in my **kitchen**. The **bathroom** is very small, so I have a **shower**, not a **bath**. I also have a **garden** where I grow flowers and vegetables. I love **living** here.

Words for talking about house and home

Word Finder

address	NOUN Your **address** is the number of the building, the name of the street, and the town or city where you live or work.
bath	NOUN A **bath** is a container that you fill with water and sit in to wash your body.
bathroom	NOUN A **bathroom** is a room that contains a bath or a shower and often a toilet.
bed	NOUN A **bed** is a piece of furniture that you lie on when you sleep.
bedroom	NOUN A **bedroom** is a room where people sleep.
chair	NOUN A **chair** is a piece of furniture for one person to sit on, with a back and four legs.
dining room	NOUN A **dining room** is a room where people eat their meals.
door	NOUN A **door** is a piece of wood, glass, or metal that fills an entrance.
flat	NOUN A **flat** is a set of rooms for living in, usually on one floor.
garden	NOUN A **garden** is an area by your house where you grow flowers and vegetables.
home	NOUN Someone's **home** is the place where they live.
house	NOUN A **house** is a building where people live.
key	NOUN A **key** is a shaped piece of metal that opens or closes a lock.
kitchen	NOUN A **kitchen** is a room that is used for cooking.
live	VERB If you **live** somewhere, you have your home in that place.
living room	NOUN The **living room** in a house is the room where people sit together and talk or watch television.
shower	NOUN A **shower** is a thing that you stand under, that covers you with water so you can wash yourself.
table	NOUN A **table** is a piece of furniture with a flat top that you put things on or sit at.
toilet	NOUN A **toilet** is a large bowl with a seat that you use when you want to get rid of waste from your body.
wall	NOUN A **wall** is one of the sides of a building or a room.
window	NOUN A **window** is a space in the wall of a building or in the side of a vehicle that has glass in it.

Exercise 1

Put the correct word or words in each gap.

| bedroom | addresses | lives | living room | dining room | kitchen | windows |

John [1]_____ in a very nice flat. He has a small [2]_____ to sleep in, and a big [3]_____ to sit in with his friends. He cooks all his meals in his [4]_____. He eats meals with his friends in the [5]_____. He can see a park from his [6]_____.

Exercise 2

Match the words with the pictures, as shown.

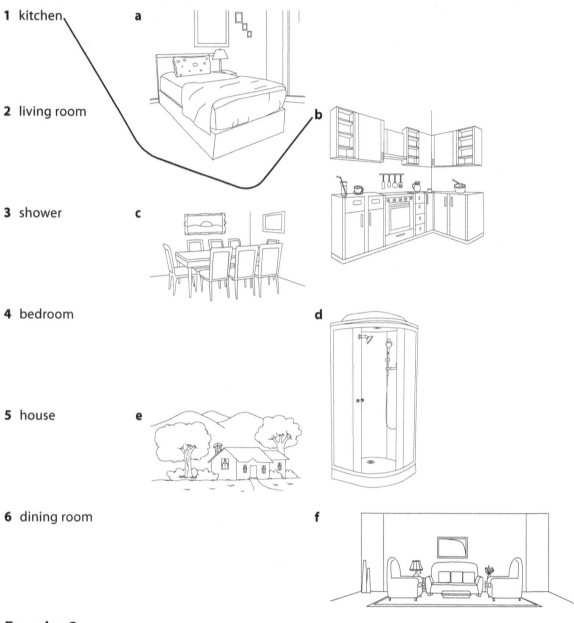

1 kitchen   **a**

2 living room   **b**

3 shower   **c**

4 bedroom   **d**

5 house   **e**

6 dining room   **f**

Exercise 3

Choose the correct word, as shown.

1 My **address** / **door** is 23, Main Street.

2 Ben is sitting outside in the **garden** / **kitchen**.

3 Put this picture on the **flat** / **wall**.

4 This house has four **kitchens** / **bedrooms**.

5 Come in and sit on the **table** / **chair**.

6 Dan is looking out of the **window** / **wall**.

Exercise 4

For each question, tick the correct answer, as shown.

1 In the living room, there are
☑ some chairs.
☐ some beds.

2 This key opens the
☐ door.
☐ table.

3 I live in a small
☐ address.
☐ flat.

4 The bedroom has white
☐ walls.
☐ showers.

5 There's a big table in the
☐ bath.
☐ kitchen.

6 There's a toilet in the
☐ living room.
☐ bathroom.

Exercise 5

Match the sentence halves.

1 I wash   a in my garden.

2 I cook   b in the bathroom.

3 I sleep   c in the bedroom.

4 I watch TV   d in the living room.

5 I have my lunch   e in the dining room.

6 I sit outside   f in the kitchen.

Exercise 6

Find the words or phrases that do not belong, as shown.

1 **Rooms**	kitchen	bathroom	window
2 **Places to live**	flat	toilet	house
3 **Things in a dining room**	garden	chair	table
4 **Rooms to wash in**	shower	dining room	bathroom
5 **Parts of a house**	address	wall	door
6 **Things in a bedroom**	bed	window	flat

Describing objects

In this picture, a girl is sitting **at** a table, looking at some pieces of **paper**. **Above** her head, there is a **big** lamp. There is a rug **under** the table.

In this picture, a boy is standing by his bedroom window, looking **outside**. The garden **below** looks lovely. The sky is **blue** and the leaves on the trees are **green**. The boy can see his dog **behind** the trees.

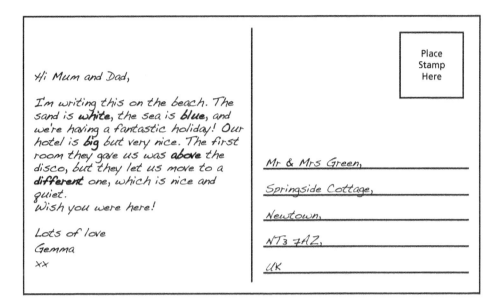

Hi Mum and Dad,

I'm writing this on the beach. The sand is **white**, the sea is **blue**, and we're having a fantastic holiday! Our hotel is **big** but very nice. The first room they gave us was **above** the disco, but they let us move to a **different** one, which is nice and quiet.
Wish you were here!

Lots of love
Gemma
xx

Place Stamp Here

Mr & Mrs Green,

Springside Cottage,

Newtown,

NT3 7AZ,

UK

Good to know!

Adjectives of size come before adjectives of colour:
He was wearing a <u>big black</u> hat.

Words that describe things

above	PREPOSITION If one thing is **above** another, it is over it or higher than it.
at	PREPOSITION You use **at** to say where something happens or is situated.
behind	PREPOSITION If something is **behind** a thing or person, it is at the back of it.
below	PREPOSITION If something is **below** something else, it is in a lower position.
big	ADJECTIVE Someone or something that is **big** is large in size.
black	ADJECTIVE Something that is **black** is the colour of the sky at night.
blue	ADJECTIVE Something that is **blue** is the colour of the sky on a sunny day.
bottom	NOUN The **bottom** of something is the lowest part of it.
brown	ADJECTIVE Something that is **brown** is the colour of earth or wood.
different	ADJECTIVE If two people or things are **different**, they are not like each other.
glass	NOUN **Glass** is used for making things such as windows and bottles.
green	ADJECTIVE Something that is **green** is the colour of grass or leaves.
important	ADJECTIVE If something is **important** to you, you feel that you must do, have, or think about it.
inside	PREPOSITION, ADVERB Something or someone that is **inside** something is in it.
object	NOUN An **object** is anything that has a fixed shape or form and that is not alive.

Word Finder

21

Word Finder	outside	PREPOSITION, ADVERB If you are **outside**, you are not in a building, but you are very close to it.
	paper	NOUN **Paper** is a material that you write on or wrap things with.
	red	ADJECTIVE Something that is **red** is the colour of blood or of a tomato.
	under	PREPOSITION If a person or a thing is **under** something, they are below it.
	white	ADJECTIVE Something that is **white** is the colour of snow or milk.
	yellow	ADJECTIVE Something that is **yellow** is the colour of lemons or butter.

Exercise 1

Find the words that do not belong, as shown.

1 Colours	black	glass	yellow
2 Positions	above	inside	red
3 Materials	under	paper	glass
4 Colours	blue	brown	below
5 Positions	big	behind	below
6 Colours	bottom	white	red
7 Positions	outside	paper	under
8 Colours	green	behind	black

Exercise 2

For each question, tick the correct answer, as shown.

1 What colour is the sky on a sunny day?
   ☑ blue
   ☐ above
   ☐ big

2 What is a window made of?
   ☐ white
   ☐ different
   ☐ glass

3 What can you write on?
   ☐ at
   ☐ green
   ☐ paper

4 Where is your neck?
   ☐ below your head
   ☐ above your head
   ☐ behind your head

5 Where is a garden usually?
   ☐ under a house
   ☐ inside a house
   ☐ outside a house

Exercise 3

Choose the correct word.

1 My new phone is very **important / outside / different** from my old phone.

2 We have four children, so we need a **big / below / behind** car.

3 If a **different / paper / glass** bottle breaks, it can cut you.

4 The **outside / above / big** walls of my house are painted white.

5 Ben stood at the **bottom / inside / under** of the stairs.

6 People's families are very **brown / above / important** to them.

Exercise 4

Put the correct word in each gap.

| inside | important | under | outside | bottom | at | paper | green |

The house was very hot, so Steven went ¹_____ into the garden. He looked around

the garden. There was a piece of ²_____ on the grass ³_____ a tree.

He looked at it. There was a name at the ⁴_____. It was the name of the country's

president, and something about him. Steven thought it was ⁵_____. He was worried.

He went back ⁶_____ the house to talk to someone about it.

Exercise 5

Write the missing word in sentence B so that it means the same as sentence A, as shown.

1 A My parents' flat is below my flat.

  B My flat is _____*above*_____ my parents' flat.

2 A The woman stood in front of a big picture.

  B There was a big picture _____ the woman.

3 A The computer was on a desk in front of everyone in the room.

  B The computer was on a desk _____ the front of the room.

4 A We didn't go outside, because it was raining.

  B We stayed _____, because it was raining.

Exercise 6

Which sentences are correct?

1 There were some red and white paper flowers in the room. ☑

2 On the table there was a boat made of glass, and there were some old clothes
  under the table. ❏

3 My new shirt is blue and bottom, and it's different from all my other shirts. ❏

4 I took a photo of some brown horses, with trees behind them. ❏

5 My mobile phone is very important to me, and I like it because it isn't below. ❏

6 There were a lot of yellow, green and black clothes on the table outside the shop. ❏

Parts of the body and describing people

Parts of the body

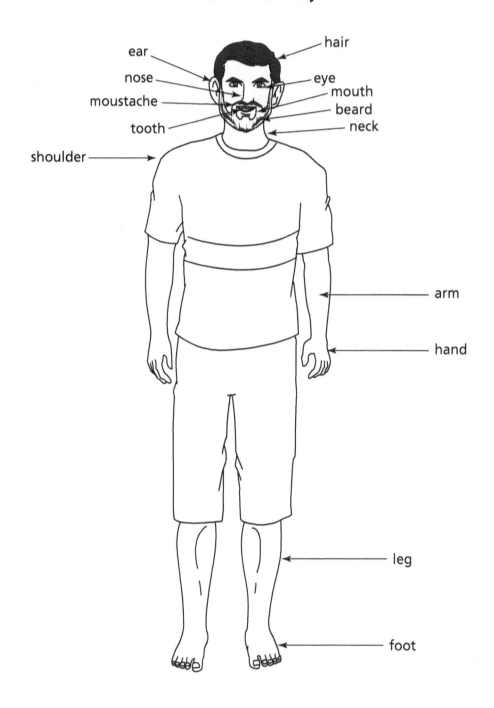

ear

nose

moustache

tooth

shoulder

hair

eye

mouth

beard

neck

arm

hand

leg

foot

Describing people

> My dad is very tall and he has short, black **hair.** He also has a short **beard.** He does a lot of sport, so he has strong **legs** and wide **shoulders.** He has brown **eyes**, a long **nose**, and quite big **ears**!

Good to know!

You can use these adjectives to talk about hair:

<u>long/short</u> hair

<u>straight/curly</u> hair

<u>dark/fair</u> hair

<u>black, brown, blonde (= yellow)</u>, <u>red, grey</u> hair

Words for talking about the different parts of the body

bald	ADJECTIVE Someone who is **bald** has no hair on the top of their head.
body	NOUN A person's **body** is all their physical parts.
face	NOUN Your **face** is the front part of your head.
head	NOUN Your **head** is the top part of your body that has your eyes, mouth and brain in it.
skin	NOUN **Skin** is the substance that covers the outside of a person's body.

Exercise 1

Rearrange the letters to find words, as shown. Use the definitions to help you.

1 hutom _____*mouth*_____ (You put food in this and use it to eat.)

2 etef _____ (You can stand on one or both of these.)

3 rase _____ (You use these to listen.)

4 eson _____ (You smell with this.)

5 dashn _____ (You can hold things with these.)

6 nisk _____ (The sun can burn this.)

Exercise 2

Which sentences are correct?

1 Your legs start at your shoulders.　❏

2 Your teeth are inside your mouth.　❏

3 Your eyes, nose and feet are all parts of your face.　❏

4 A bald man is a man with no hair on his head.　❏

5 Your skin is something inside your body.　❏

6 A moustache grows between a man's nose and his mouth.　❏

Exercise 3

Complete the sentences by writing one word in each gap.

1 Gina has dark _____ that goes down to her shoulders.

2 Terry is bald, but he has a grey moustache and _____.

3 Your arms and legs are part of your _____.

4 How long can you stand on one _____?

5 Some people need glasses because their _____ are weak.

6 We hold a pen in one _____ when we write.

Exercise 4

Are the highlighted words correct or incorrect in the sentences?

1 The sun was hot, so the man wore a hat on his **bald** ❏ head.

2 Freddie has got long **legs** ❏, so he can run very fast.

3 The dog stood on two **hands** ❏ and tried to get the food on the table.

4 When the lion opened its mouth, you could see its **teeth** ❏.

5 It was cold, so Joe wore his coat and a scarf round his **arms** ❏.

6 Rachel closed her **eyes** ❏ and went to sleep.

6

Clothes

For school, I wear a dark blue **skirt** and a white **shirt**. In winter, I wear a blue **sweater**. I wear black **shoes** and long white **socks**.

At the weekend, I like to wear comfortable **clothes**. I usually wear **jeans** and a **T-shirt**.

For school, I wear black **trousers** and a white **shirt**. We also have to wear a **jacket**, even in summer when it is hot!

At the weekend, I love to go to the beach and I usually wear **shorts** and a **T-shirt.** I always wear my **watch** because my mum gets angry if I'm late for dinner!

When I go outside in winter, I **put on** a warm **coat**, and I always wear a **hat** and **gloves** to keep my hands warm.

For work, I usually wear a **dress** with a **jacket**. I really love fashionable **shoes** because they make me feel good!

Good to know!

Remember that _trousers, shorts_ are plural. You must use a plural verb with them:

My trousers _are_ too big for me.

His shorts _were_ too small for him.

The word _clothes_ is also plural. There is no singular form:

All my _clothes_ were in the suitcase.

Words for talking about clothes

clothes	PLURAL NOUN **Clothes** are the things that people wear, such as shirts, coats, trousers, and dresses.
coat	NOUN A **coat** is a piece of clothing that you wear over other clothes when you go outside.
dress	NOUN A **dress** is a piece of woman's or girl's clothing that covers the body and part of the legs.
glove	NOUN **Gloves** are pieces of clothing you wear to keep your hands warm.
hat	NOUN A **hat** is a thing that you wear on your head.
jacket	NOUN A **jacket** is a short coat with long sleeves.
jeans	PLURAL NOUN **Jeans** are trousers that are made of strong blue cloth.
put on	PHRASAL VERB If you **put on** clothes, you start to wear them.
scarf	NOUN A **scarf** is a piece of cloth that you wear around your neck or head.
shirt	NOUN A **shirt** is a piece of clothing, with a collar and buttons, that you wear on the top part of your body.
shoe	NOUN **Shoes** are things that you wear on your feet.
shorts	PLURAL NOUN **Shorts** are trousers with very short legs.
skirt	NOUN A **skirt** is a piece of woman's or girl's clothing that hangs down and covers part of the legs.
sock	NOUN **Socks** are pieces of clothing that you wear on your feet, inside your shoes.
sweater	NOUN A **sweater** is a warm piece of clothing that covers the top part of your body and your arms.
trousers	PLURAL NOUN **Trousers** are a piece of clothing that covers your legs.
T-shirt	NOUN A **T-shirt** is a cotton shirt with no buttons and short sleeves.
umbrella	NOUN An **umbrella** is a long stick with a cover that you use to protect yourself from the rain.
watch	NOUN A **watch** is a small clock that you wear on your arm.
wear	VERB When you **wear** clothes, you have them on your body.

Word Finder

Exercise 1

For each question, tick the correct answer.

1 What do you put on in the mornings?
❏ Clothes.
❏ An umbrella.

2 When do you wear a coat?
❏ In hot weather.
❏ In cold weather.

3 Where do you wear a watch?
❏ On my arm.
❏ On my head.

4 What do you wear at the beach?
❏ Gloves.
❏ Shorts.

5 When do you wear a T-shirt?
❏ When you go swimming.
❏ When you play tennis.

6 What can you put on with jeans?
❏ A skirt.
❏ A shirt.

Exercise 2

Match the words with the pictures.

1 scarf

2 dress

3 shirt

4 skirt

5 watch

6 shoes

a

b

c

d

e

f

Exercise 3

Rearrange the letters to find words. Use the definitions to help you.

1 snaje _____ (These trousers are usually blue or black.)

2 triks _____ (A woman can wear this.)

3 lebruaml _____ (You use this in wet weather.)

4 tajcek _____ (Put this on when you are cold.)

5 lestoch _____ (You wear these every day.)

6 sthriT- _____ (You can wear this at the beach.)

Exercise 4

Put the correct word in each gap, as shown.

watch | umbrella | shorts | gloves | hat | socks

1 You wear these on your hands. _____*gloves*_____

2 You put these on your feet. _____

3 You use this when it rains. _____

4 You wear these to play football. _____

5 You put this on your head. _____

6 You use this to tell the time. _____

Exercise 5

Put the correct word in each gap.

shirt | sweater | gloves | hat | shoes | jacket

Hi Tim,

Thanks for your email. I'm happy you like football! I play on Saturdays. I always wear shorts and a red football [1]_____ with the number 7 on it.

Of course, I wear sports [2]_____ on my feet. When it is cold, I wear [3]_____ on my hands and a [4]_____ on my head. I wear a [5]_____ too, to be warm. When we finish. I put on my [6]_____ and go home.

See you,

Tom

Exercise 6

Put each sentence into the correct order.

1 socks / put on / before / you / your shoes / your / .

_____

2 beach / shorts / I / at / the / wear / .

_____

3 an / umbrella / take / because / raining / it's / .

_____

4 my mum / I'm / a scarf / for / her birthday / buying / .

_____

5 putting on / his coat / Sam is / because / cold / it's / .

_____

6 wearing / her / dress / new / is / Pam / .

_____

7

Talking about people

This is my sister Holly. She is 24, and she has two children – a **little boy** called Zak and a **baby girl** called Chloe. Holly is a great mum and she is very **happy** with her **young** family.

This is my mum. She's nearly 60 and I think she is really **beautiful**. Mum is a teacher. It's a hard job, and she's sometimes **tired** when she comes home from work.

This is my brother James. James is very **tall** and he loves playing basketball. He's also very **clever**. He's at university studying politics. He's always talking about politics, which I find quite **boring**!

This is my grandma. She's quite **old**, and she's very **short**! I love visiting her because she's so **nice**, and she makes great cakes! She lives on her own, but she says she's not **sad** about it because we visit her a lot and she has lots of friends.

Words for talking about people

Word Finder

adult	NOUN An **adult** is a fully-grown person or animal.
baby	NOUN A **baby** is a very young child.
beautiful	ADJECTIVE A **beautiful** person is very nice to look at.
boring	ADJECTIVE Someone or something that is **boring** is not at all interesting.
boy	NOUN A **boy** is a male child.
clever	ADJECTIVE Someone who is **clever** is intelligent and can think and understand quickly.
girl	NOUN A **girl** is a female child.
happy	ADJECTIVE Someone who is **happy** feels pleased.
little	ADJECTIVE Something that is **little** is small.
man	NOUN A **man** is an adult male human.
nice	ADJECTIVE If something is **nice**, it is attractive, pleasant, or enjoyable.
old	ADJECTIVE Someone who is **old** has lived for many years and is not young.
sad	ADJECTIVE If you are **sad**, you feel unhappy.
short	ADJECTIVE Someone who is **short** is not tall.
slim	ADJECTIVE If you are **slim**, your body is thin in an attractive way.
small	ADJECTIVE If something is **small**, it is not large.
tall	ADJECTIVE If someone is **tall**, they are higher than most other people.
tired	ADJECTIVE If you are **tired**, you feel that you want to rest or sleep.
woman	NOUN A **woman** is an adult female human being.
young	ADJECTIVE A **young** person, animal, or plant has not lived for very long.

Exercise 1

For each question, tick the correct answer.

1 The opposite of old is
 ❏ short.
 ❏ young.
 ❏ sad.

2 The opposite of tall is
 ❏ happy.
 ❏ slim.
 ❏ short.

3 The opposite of big is
 ❏ small.
 ❏ tall.
 ❏ nice.

4 The opposite of interesting is
 ❏ clever.
 ❏ boring.
 ❏ slim.

5 The opposite of sad is
 ❏ happy.
 ❏ short.
 ❏ beautiful.

6 The opposite of stupid is
 ❏ happy.
 ❏ small.
 ❏ clever.

Exercise 2

Match the sentence halves.

1 Gloria's mother is a   a go to the party.

2 My sister is ten   b because it was hungry.

3 You have to be tall   c but she's still very small.

4 Cass was too tired to   d when you are young.

5 The baby was crying   e very beautiful woman.

6 It's best to learn languages   f to play basketball.

Exercise 3

Choose the correct word.

1 Gabrielle doesn't eat chocolate because she wants to keep **short / slim / small**.

2 Ravi wants to be a doctor, but I don't think he's **tired / boring / clever** enough.

3 Lily's lucky – her boyfriend is really **nice / sad / tired**.

4 I think Eva is more **little / old / beautiful** than her sister.

5 I hate talking to Mr Bush because he's so **happy / boring / tired**.

6 My aunt is too **old / clever / slim** to have children now.

Exercise 4

Put the correct word in each gap.

old | happy | young | clever | man | short

My grandfather

When I was ¹_____, my grandfather and I played football together a lot. His legs are quite ²_____, but he could run very fast. I was always ³_____ when I was with him.

My grandfather is quite ⁴_____ now, so he can't run around any more. I still visit him every week, and we often play chess. He's very ⁵_____, so he usually wins. I don't mind, because he's such a nice ⁶_____ and I love spending time with him.

Exercise 5

Complete the sentences by writing one word in each gap.

adults | young | woman | tired | girls | baby

1 This club is for _____ only.

2 I need to go to bed. I'm really _____.

3 Kazuo's wife is a very nice _____.

4 My friend Katie had a _____ last week.

5 Poppy is too _____ to walk to school alone.

6 Bella and Stella are the only two _____ in the children's football club in our town.

Exercise 6

Match the words with the pictures.

1 tall

a

2 old

b

3 slim

c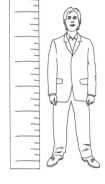

4 short

d

5 tired

e

6 happy

f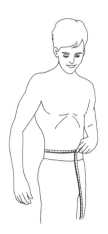

8

School and university

 Every morning, I take my little sister to **school** near our house. Sometimes I go into the **classroom** with her to look at her work. She is **learning** to **read** and she loves **books**.

 I like most of the **teachers** at my school, but some of them give us too much **homework**. My favourite **subject** is history because we have a great teacher who knows how to make her **lessons** really interesting.

 I am a **student** at the **university** here in Liverpool. I am **studying** maths. I have important **exams** at the end of the year, so I'm going to have to study very hard for them!

Make sure you use the right verbs with the phrases.

Verb	phrase
go to	school/university
do/take	a test/an exam/a course
have	lessons
do	your homework
study	English, maths, etc.

Good to know!

Paper is an uncountable noun. You cannot put 'a' in front of it. If you want to talk about one piece, you can say a piece of paper.

Words for talking about school and university

board	NOUN A **board** is the flat black or white surface in a classroom that a teacher writes on.
book	NOUN A **book** is a number of pieces of paper, usually with words printed on them, that are fastened together and fixed inside a cover.
class	NOUN A **class** is a group of students who learn at school together.
classroom	NOUN A **classroom** is a room in a school where lessons take place.
course	NOUN A **course** is a series of lessons on a particular subject.
dictionary	NOUN A **dictionary** is a book in which the words and phrases of a language are listed, together with their meanings.
exam	NOUN An **exam** is a formal test that you take to show your knowledge of a subject.
homework	NOUN **Homework** is school work that teachers give to students to do at home.

Word Finder

learn	VERB If you **learn** something, you get knowledge or a skill by studying, training, or through experience.
lesson	NOUN A **lesson** is a time when you learn about a particular subject.
paper	NOUN **Paper** is a material that you write on.
read	VERB When you **read** a book or a story, you look at the written words and understand them.
school	NOUN A **school** is a place where people go to learn.
student	NOUN A **student** is a person who is studying at a school, college, or university.
study	VERB If you **study**, you spend time learning about a particular subject.
subject	NOUN A **subject** is an area of knowledge that you study in school or college.
teacher	NOUN A **teacher** is someone whose job is to teach students in a school.
test	NOUN A **test** is a series of questions you must answer to show how much you know about something.
university	NOUN A **university** is a place where you can study after leaving school.

Word Finder

Exercise 1

Complete the sentences by writing one word in each gap.

board | subject | lessons | learn | exam | school

1 What _____ is your sister studying at university?

2 I had a maths _____ last week.

3 I don't like my French teacher. His _____ are boring.

4 The teacher wrote the answers on the _____ .

5 Ross and I were at _____ together.

6 Children don't _____ the names of kings and queens now.

Exercise 2

Put the correct word in each gap.

read | classroom | learned | books | teacher | lessons

My first school

I started school when I was five. My [1]_____ was called Miss Walton. She was kind, and her [2]_____ were fun. Our [3]_____ was big, and we had low tables and small chairs.

We soon [4]_____ to [5]_____ and write. I loved the big [6]_____ with lots of pictures.

Exercise 3

Match the sentence halves.

1 Music and maths are my favourite   **a** homework.

2 All the students are working hard for their   **b** subjects.

3 If you sit at the back of the classroom, you won't see the   **c** board.

4 Every evening Maggie spends an hour doing her   **d** university.

5 I liked chemistry and physics at school, so I studied it at   **e** exams.

6 Everyone studying history must also take an English   **f** course.

Exercise 4

Are the highlighted words correct or incorrect in the sentences?

1 Anna isn't very happy at **class** ⊠.

2 I can't find this word in my **dictionary** ❏.

3 Adam is having piano **school** ❏.

4 I am going to **university** ❏ next year.

5 I did all my **homework** ❏ at the weekend.

6 There are 30 students in my **lesson** ❏.

Exercise 5

Put each sentence into the correct order, as shown.

1 subject / what / your / favourite / is / ?

   What is your favourite subject?

2 students / the / ten / course / took / French / .

   _____

3 is studying / my / at / brother / history / university / .

   _____

4 give / English teacher / us / doesn't / much / our / homework / .

   _____

5 have / we / spelling / going to / a / test / are / ?

   _____

6 to / I'd / to sing / like / learn / .

   _____

9

Sports and leisure

I play basketball.

I play tennis.

I go fishing.

I play football.

I go swimming.

I go sailing.

To: Alex Harris
From: Ben Jones
Subject: Update

Hi Alex

Did Tom tell you that I'm **captain** of the **football** team now? We've got our first **game** on Sunday, at the **sports centre**. I'm really excited! We've got a lot of good new **players**, so I hope we can **play** well!

See you soon.
Ben

To: Ben Jones
From: Alex Harris
Subject: Congratulations!

Hi Ben

Good to hear from you, and pleased to hear you're **captain** now – congratulations! I've been doing a lot of **swimming** recently. I go to the **pool** most days before college. I have a big **race** next weekend.

If you're free, perhaps you could come?
Alex

Words for talking about sports and leisure

ball	NOUN A **ball** is a round object that is used in games such as tennis and football.
basketball	NOUN **Basketball** is a game in which players try to throw a large ball through a round net hanging from a high metal ring.
captain	NOUN The **captain** of a sports team is its leader.
fishing	NOUN **Fishing** is the sport of catching fish.
football	NOUN **Football** is a game for two teams who try to kick the ball into a net at the other end of the field.
game	NOUN A **game** is an activity or a sport in which you try to win against someone.
leisure	NOUN **Leisure** is the time when you do not have to work and can do things that you enjoy.
match	NOUN A **match** is an organized sports game.
play	VERB When you **play** a game or a sport, you take part in it.
player	NOUN A **player** is a person who takes part in a sport or game.
pool	NOUN A **pool** or **swimming pool** is a large hole in the ground that is filled with water for people to swim in.
quiz	NOUN A **quiz** is a competition in which someone tests your knowledge by asking you questions.
race	NOUN A **race** is a competition to see who is the fastest.
run	NOUN If you go for a **run**, you run to take exercise.
sailing	NOUN **Sailing** is the activity or sport of sailing boats.
sport	NOUN **Sports** are games and other activities that need physical effort and skill.
sports centre	NOUN A **sports centre** is a building where you can go to do sports and other activities.
swim	VERB When you **swim**, you move through water by making movements with your arms and legs.
swimming	NOUN **Swimming** is the activity of swimming, especially as a sport or for pleasure.
tennis	NOUN **Tennis** is a game where players use rackets to hit a ball across a net between them.

Word Finder

Exercise 1

Match the sentence halves.

1	How often do you go	**a**	the race?
2	What do you do at the	**b**	swimming?
3	Do you often play	**c**	the football team?
4	How many runners were in	**d**	basketball?
5	Who is the captain of	**e**	sports centre?

Exercise 2

Choose the correct word.

1 We can't play **game / tennis** without a ball.

2 Would you like to go **basketball / sailing** with me at the weekend?

3 My class had a **quiz / match** about football last Friday.

4 I usually play **sport / football** at the sports centre.

5 My brother can swim very fast, so he always wins when we have a **race / game**.

6 Let's go for a **player / run** tomorrow morning.

Exercise 3

Put each sentence into the correct order.

1 after / I'd like / swimming / go / school / to / .

_____

2 wants / the match / to / the captain / the players / win / .

_____

3 game / my sister and I / a good / had / of / tennis / .

_____

4 sailing / I prefer / basketball / my father goes / but / playing / .

_____

5 the sports / a good / there's / centre / at / pool / .

_____

6 go / but the young men / the old men / play / fishing / football / .

_____

Exercise 4

Which sentences are correct?

1 I like watching a good football match on television. ❏

2 Do you play sport at your school? ❏

3 I don't enjoy ball games. ❏

4 The swimming is my favourite sport. ❏

5 Who is the best player in your basketball team? ❏

6 I played a race at the sports centre. ❏

Work and jobs

Jobs

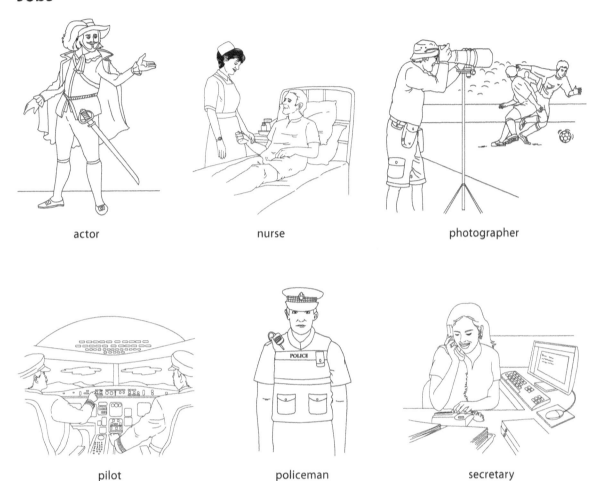

actor   nurse   photographer

pilot   policeman   secretary

Talking about work

I work for a **company** that makes and sells televisions. We have **offices** in several countries around the world, and I am the **manager** of the office in London. Sometimes I travel to China to visit our **factory** there and talk to the **workers**. I love my **job**.

Words for talking about work and jobs

actor	NOUN An **actor** is someone whose job is acting in plays or movies.
artist	NOUN An **artist** is someone who draws, paints, or creates other works of art.
businessman	NOUN A **businessman** is a man who works in business.
company	NOUN A **company** is a business that sells goods or services.
doctor	NOUN A **doctor** is a person whose job is to treat people who are sick or injured.
factory	NOUN A **factory** is a large building where people use machines to make goods.
farmer	NOUN A **farmer** is a person who works on a farm.
guide	NOUN A **guide** is someone who shows tourists around places such as museums or cities.
job	NOUN A **job** is the work that someone does to earn money.
manager	NOUN A **manager** is a person who controls all or part of a business or an organization.
nurse	NOUN A **nurse** is a person whose job is to care for people who are sick.
office	NOUN An **office** is a place where people work sitting at a desk.
photographer	NOUN A **photographer** is someone who takes photographs as a job.
pilot	NOUN A **pilot** is a person who controls an aircraft.
policeman	NOUN A **policeman** is a man who is a member of the police force.
policewoman	NOUN A **policewoman** is a woman who is a member of the police force.
secretary	NOUN A **secretary** is a person whose job is to type letters, answer the telephone, and do other office work.
singer	NOUN A **singer** is a person who sings, especially as a job.
teacher	NOUN A **teacher** is someone whose job is to teach students in a school.
work	1 VERB People who **work** have a job and earn money for it. 2 NOUN Your **work** is the job that you do to earn money.
worker	NOUN **Workers** are people who work, who are below the level of a manager.

Exercise 1

Choose the correct word.

1 During the university holidays, I work as a **guide / job** for foreign visitors to our city.

2 My sister loves the theatre so she wants to be an **actor / artist** when she leaves school.

3 My brother works in a bank, but he'd like to start his own **office / company** one day.

4 It's hard to find a **work / job** in this part of the country.

5 My uncle is a **worker / businessman**. He started his company in 2005.

6 The **pilot / manager** of the travel company helped me to get cheap tickets for my flights.

Exercise 2

Match the words with the pictures.

1 doctor   **a**

2 teacher   **b**

3 artist   **c**

4 farmer   **d**

5 guide   **e**

6 singer   **f**

Exercise 3

Match the sentence halves.

1 Photographers   **a** work in factories, shops, banks and many other kinds of company.
2 Managers   **b** help make things for their company to sell.
3 Pilots   **c** take pictures of all kinds of people and places.
4 Nurses   **d** prepare their lessons very carefully.
5 Good teachers   **e** work with sick people in hospital.
6 Factory workers   **f** work on planes or helicopters.

Exercise 4

Put the correct word in each gap.

| pilot | farmer | actor | photographer | nurse | doctor | teacher | singer |

1 classroom _____

2 hospital _____ _____

3 airport _____

4 theatre _____ _____

5 fields _____

6 newspaper _____

Exercise 5

Rearrange the letters to find words. Use the definitions to help you.

1 nameciwolop _____ (She can give you help.)

2 angream _____ (This person gives jobs to other workers.)

3 crathee _____ (A class learns from this person.)

4 marref _____ (This person grows food for us.)

5 ugdie _____ (This person takes tourists round interesting places.)

6 repoothpargh _____ (This person uses a camera at work.)

Exercise 6

Are the highlighted words correct or incorrect in the sentences?

1 After the accident, the **police officers** ❑ spoke to all the drivers.

2 We keep the important business papers in this **secretary** ❑.

3 Our house is clean and tidy because we have a **worker** ❑ two days a week.

4 I want to change my **job** ❑ and get more money so I can travel.

5 The **office** ❑ manager is on holiday this week.

6 I telephoned a **factory** ❑ when we had a problem with our car and he came to fix it.

11

Daily routines

In the morning, I'm often late for school.

I get up. I get dressed. I go to school. I finish school.

After school, I have more time so I help my mum.

I go shopping. My mum has a rest. I do the cooking. I do the cleaning.

At the weekend, I can relax.

I watch TV. I go out. I meet friends. We go swimming.

Make sure you use the right verbs with the phrases.

Verb	phrase
do	the cooking/the cleaning
drink	coffee/tea
drive	to work/to school
eat	a sandwich lunch
finish	work/school
get	up dressed
go	out shopping/swimming to school/to work
have	a rest/a shower/a walk coffee/tea lunch/breakfast
listen	to music
meet	friends
play	tennis
put	the book (on the table, on the shelf, in the bag)
wash	your hands
watch	TV

Exercise 1

Choose the correct word.

1 Maria **listens / meets / drives** to music every day.

2 She **does / watches / sleeps** TV in the morning.

3 She **drinks / plays / eats** a sandwich for lunch.

4 She **goes / finishes / has** to work by bus.

5 She **gets / does / puts** the cleaning at the weekend.

6 She **goes / sleeps / has** a rest in the afternoon.

Exercise 2

Put the correct word or phrase in each gap.

| get up | drive | In the morning | have | have | play |

At Carbeen Hotel, you can have a wonderful holiday. If you come by car, you can
¹_____ just five miles and see the beautiful lakes. We have twenty comfortable
rooms. When you ²_____, you can sit on your balcony and ³_____
breakfast there or go to our restaurant. ⁴_____, you can ⁵_____ a walk
in our garden. In the afternoon, you can ⁶_____ tennis or relax in our lounge.

Exercise 3

Choose the correct word.

1 I go **to / on / in** work at 8 o'clock.

2 Can you put my book **in / on / to** the table, please?

3 I **have / put / go** shopping at the weekend.

4 I like reading a book **in / on / at** the morning.

5 Hurry up! **Have / Get / Put** dressed.

6 I'm tired. I'm going to have **the / an / a** rest.

Exercise 4

Which sentences are correct?

1 I think I put my phone in my bag. ❏

2 Are you having a lunch now? ❏

3 What time do you want to go to the shopping? ❏

4 I'll have a shower and then we can leave. ❏

5 Can Tom meet us in morning before we have class? ❏

6 Would you like to have coffee with us later? ❏

Exercise 5

Complete the text by writing one word in each gap.

At the weekend, I get [1] _____ late, at about 10 a.m. [2] _____ the morning, I read the newspaper and have breakfast. After lunch, I [3] _____ shopping and then come back home. I go [4] _____ with my friends at about 8 p.m. There is a very good restaurant near my apartment, so we sometimes go there. I don't [5] _____ meat and that restaurant has delicious vegetarian food. I go home late on Saturday night and sometimes [6] _____ TV before I go to bed.

12

Words that are used together (collocations)

Collocations are words that go together in a natural way. When you learn a word, you need to learn the words that go with it to make a sentence.

Many collocations are formed with a verb and a noun. It is very important to use the right verb, and a good dictionary will help you with this. For example, you say **watch TV**, NOT ~~see TV~~ or ~~look at the TV~~.

Here are some other useful collocations formed with a verb and a noun:

*I **have a shower** before breakfast.*
*We usually **have dinner** at eight o'clock.*
*I **left school** when I was 16.*
*I love **playing football**.*

There are also other kinds of collocations. Here are some more useful ones:

*What do you do in your **free time**? (adjective + noun)*
*I'll give you my **phone number**. (noun + noun)*
*When did you **get married**? (verb + adjective)*
*It's time to **go home**. (verb + adverb)*

Look at the different collocations:

> ## *What gets you up in the mornings?*
>
> **Do you enjoy your job?**
> I love it! The only thing I don't love is that
> I **start work** at six o'clock in the morning,
> so I have to get up very early.
>
> **How did you become a radio journalist?**
> I'm very lucky! I **got a job** as an
> assistant at my local radio station after
> I **left school**. One day, one of journalists
> asked me to present a show with him, as a
> one-off. That's how it all started!
>
> **What do you do in your free time?**
> I enjoy **playing the piano**, and I **read**
> a lot of **books**, but often I'm so tired, that
> I just **watch TV**.

Words that are used together

capital letter	NOUN A **capital letter** is the form of a letter that is written at the beginning of a sentence.
email address	NOUN An **email address** is the letters and symbols you need to send an email to someone.
fast food	NOUN **Fast food** is hot food that is served quickly in a restaurant.
free time	NOUN **Free time** is the time you have when you are not working or studying and can do what you like.
full stop	NOUN A **full stop** is the mark (.) used in writing at the end of a sentence when it is not a question or an exclamation.
get married	VERB If you **get married**, you become someone's husband or wife.
go to work	VERB If you **go to work**, you go somewhere to do your job.
phone number	NOUN Your **phone number** is the number that people use to call you on the phone.
question mark	NOUN A **question mark** is the mark (?) that is used in writing at the end of a question.

Word Finder

Exercise 1

Rearrange the letters to find words. Use the clues to help you.

1 traugi _____ (You can play the _____.)

2 bestfraak _____ (You can have _____ at 8am.)

3 wherso _____ (You can have a _____ in the morning.)

4 boatflol _____ (You can play _____.)

5 dreamir _____ (You can get _____.)

6 colosh _____ (You can leave _____ when you are 16 years old.)

Exercise 2

Match the two parts.

1 play   **a** the piano

2 question   **b** mark

3 full   **c** letter

4 free   **d** time

5 capital   **e** stop

Exercise 3

Put the correct word in each gap.

piano	breakfast	football	shower	school	job	time

I left ¹_____ a few months ago, and I can't get a ²_____, so I have plenty of free ³_____. I have ⁴_____ quite late, then I have a ⁵_____ and get dressed. I usually play the ⁶_____ in the afternoon, and see my friends in the evening.

Exercise 4

Complete the sentences by writing one word in each gap.

| mark | new | got | capital | free | have | be | start |

1 My best friend _____ married last Saturday, and I went to her wedding.

2 When you write something, every sentence begins with a _____ letter.

3 I'm going to _____ work next week.

4 Would you like to _____ a drink before you go home?

5 Do you play much sport in your _____ time?

6 A question _____ at the end of a sentence shows that you want an answer.

Exercise 5

Which sentences are correct?

1 I'm going to go home and read a book. ❏

2 You need to start every sentence with a capital letter and end with a full mark. ❏

3 Judy goes to the work by bus, but she wants to start cycling. ❏

4 I don't often eat fast food because it isn't very good for you. ❏

5 My whole family had a dinner in a Chinese restaurant yesterday evening. ❏

6 I learned to play the piano when I was a child, but I stopped after two years because I preferred watching TV. ❏

Exercise 6

Complete the sentences by writing a phrase in each gap.

| go home | play football | fast food | phone number |
| get a job | leave school | email address |

1 I'd like to send you some information, but I haven't got your _____.

2 How often do you and your friends _____ in the park?

3 People who are very good at something can usually _____ quite easily.

4 I'll give you my _____ so you can call me if there are any problems.

5 This is a great party, so I don't want to _____.

6 Do many people in your country go to university when they _____?

13

Time

On **Monday evening**, I went to the theatre.

On **Tuesday** at **half past two**, I went to the dentist.

On **Wednesday morning**, my friend Rosa came for coffee.

On **Thursday**, it was Dan's **birthday**.

On **Friday afternoon**, I had my piano lesson.

Emma and Jamie stayed with us on **Saturday night**.

I played tennis with Julie at **ten o'clock** on **Sunday**.

That's what happened last **week**!

Good to know!

Remember that you use <u>on</u> before days of the week, and <u>at</u> before times:

It is my birthday <u>on Sunday</u>.

I will meet you <u>at three o'clock</u>.

Words for talking about time

afternoon	NOUN The **afternoon** is the part of each day that begins at lunchtime and ends at about six o'clock.
birthday	NOUN Your **birthday** is the day of the year that you were born.
day	NOUN A **day** is one period of 24 hours.
evening	NOUN The **evening** is the part of each day between the end of the afternoon and midnight.
Friday	NOUN **Friday** is the day after Thursday and before Saturday.
half past	NOUN **Half past** a particular hour is 30 minutes after that time.
late	1 ADJECTIVE If someone or something is **late**, they arrive or happen after the time they should start or happen. 2 ADVERB **Late** means after the time that something should start or happen.
minute	NOUN A **minute** is a unit of time that lasts 60 seconds.
Monday	NOUN **Monday** is the day after Sunday and before Tuesday.
morning	NOUN The **morning** is the part of each day between the time that people usually wake up and lunchtime.
night	NOUN **Night** is the time when it is dark outside, and most people sleep.
o'clock	ADVERB **O'clock** is used after numbers from one to twelve to say what time it is.
Saturday	NOUN **Saturday** is the day after Friday and before Sunday.
Sunday	NOUN **Sunday** is the day after Saturday and before Monday.
Thursday	NOUN **Thursday** is the day after Wednesday and before Friday.
time	NOUN **Time** is something that we measure in minutes, hours, days, and years.
today	ADVERB You use **today** when you are talking about the actual day on which you are speaking or writing.
Tuesday	NOUN **Tuesday** is the day after Monday and before Wednesday.
Wednesday	NOUN **Wednesday** is the day after Tuesday and before Thursday.
week	NOUN A **week** is a period of seven days.

Word Finder

Exercise 1

Match the sentence halves.

1 When is your

2 Can you come to my house at half

3 I'm going on holiday

4 The football match is on Saturday at

5 What time

6 I'll phone you this

a on Monday.

b afternoon.

c two o'clock.

d is it, please?

e birthday party?

f past four?

Exercise 2

Put each sentence into the correct order.

1 late / you / are / why / ?

_____

2 birthday / it / on / Wednesday / is / my / .

_____

3 you / are / going / time / to / what / today / work / ?

_____

4 six / is / English / fifteen / at / class / our / .

_____

5 you / on / free / Sunday / are / ?

_____

6 my / party / come / to / like / you / would / to / ?

_____

Exercise 3

Find the words or phrases that do not belong, as shown.

1 **Days**	Wednesday	evening	Thursday	Saturday
2 **Parts of the day**	morning	afternoon	late	night
3 **Numbers 1 to 10**	one	eight	two	eleven
4 **Numbers 11 to 20**	thirty	nineteen	fifteen	twelve
5 **Time**	It's 2.15 p.m.	It's 3.30 p.m.	It's 16.20.	It's 7.40 p.m.
6 **Numbers**	twenty-two	thirty-five	forty-four	fifty-five

Exercise 4

Find the wrong or extra word in each sentence.

1 I'm going to the cinema on the Saturday.

2 Jack's birthday party is on at 8 o'clock.

3 The bus is late on today.

4 Let's have a coffee together in a for minute.

5 There's a good film on TV tonight at half past to six.

6 What date is it your birthday?

Exercise 5

Write the word for the number in brackets to complete each sentence.

1 The film is _____ (90) minutes long.

2 He was on the phone for _____ (45) minutes.

3 The bus comes at _____ (12.20).

4 Does the party start at _____ (8.30)?

5 The flight is _____ (7) hours long.

6 You're _____ (20) minutes late!

14

Transport

Make sure you use the right words together.

buy a ticket	I **bought** a ticket at the station.
go **by** bicycle, bus, car, coach, plane, taxi, train	I went to Paris **by** train. We decided to travel **by** plane.
get/take/catch a bus, coach, train, plane	He **got** a coach to London. I **took** a bus to the town centre. We **caught** a plane to Rio.
get/take a taxi	We **got** a taxi to the station. It's best to **take** a taxi to the hotel.
get on/get off a bus, coach, train	I **got on** the bus at the end of the road. Make sure you **get off** the train in Cambridge.
go on a trip	We **went on** a school trip to Paris.
ride a bicycle	I often **ride** my bicycle to work.

Good to know!

Although it is possible to say _drive a car_, it is much more common to use _drive_ on its own:

Maria _drove_ all the way to Manchester.

Shall I _drive?_

You can also use the name of a person after _drive_.

I have to _drive_ Max to the station.

To: Helen Shapcott

From: Jeremy Maxwell

Subject: Paris trip

Hi Helen

Everything is arranged for your Paris meeting.

I will send your **tickets** to you this morning. You will need to be at St Pancras **station** by 8.30, and the **train** arrives in Paris at around 12 o'clock.

Jean Dubost will meet you and **drive** you to your hotel, which is quite **near** the office. Ask the hotel to call a **taxi** for you.

Have a good **trip**!

Jeremy

Words for talking about transport

bicycle	NOUN A **bicycle** is a vehicle with two wheels. You ride it by sitting on it and using your legs to make the wheels turn.
bus	NOUN A **bus** is a large motor vehicle that carries passengers and stops often for people to get on and off.
car	NOUN A **car** is a motor vehicle with space for about five people.
car park	NOUN A **car park** is an area of ground or a building where people can leave their cars for a period of time.
coach	NOUN A **coach** is a large motor vehicle that carries passengers, usually for long journeys.
drive	VERB When you **drive**, you control the movement and direction of a car or other vehicle.
far	ADVERB If one place, thing, or person is **far** away from another, there is a great distance between them.
go	VERB When you **go** somewhere, you move or travel there.
near	PREPOSITION If something is **near** a place, a thing, or a person, it is a short distance from them.
plane	NOUN A **plane** is a vehicle with wings and engines that can fly.
ride	VERB When you **ride** a bicycle or a horse, you sit on it, control it, and travel on it.
road	NOUN A **road** is a long piece of hard ground that vehicles travel on.
station	NOUN A **station** is a place where trains stop so that people can get on or off.
take	VERB If you **take** a vehicle, you use it to go from one place to another.
taxi	NOUN A **taxi** is a car with its driver, who you pay to take you where you want to go.
ticket	NOUN A **ticket** is a small piece of paper that shows that you have paid to go somewhere or to do something.
train	NOUN A **train** is a long vehicle that is pulled by an engine.
transport	NOUN **Transport** refers to any type of vehicle that you can travel in.
trip	NOUN A **trip** is a journey that you make to a particular place.

Word Finder

Exercise 1

Match the sentence halves.

1 He rides

2 The supermarket is not

3 Oh no! The car park

4 I don't want to go there

5 The ticket is cheaper

6 Go down this road and you will see

a if you buy it online.

b the post office on the left.

c far from here.

d his bicycle to work.

e is full.

f by coach.

Exercise 2

Match the words with the pictures.

1 bus   **a**

2 car

b

3 plane   **c**

4 taxi

d

5 train   **e**

6 bicycle

f

Exercise 3

For each question, tick the correct answer.

1 You can fly in this.
- ❑ a car
- ❑ a plane
- ❑ a train

2 This takes passengers and goes on the road.
- ❑ a coach
- ❑ a train
- ❑ a bicycle

3 This goes on the road and you pay the driver.
- ❑ a plane
- ❑ a train
- ❑ a taxi

4 You ride this.
- ❑ a bicycle
- ❑ a car
- ❑ a plane

5 You don't need a ticket for this.
- ❑ a coach
- ❑ a car
- ❑ a train

6 You get on the train here.
- ❑ a car park
- ❑ an airport
- ❑ a station

Exercise 4

Put the correct word in each gap.

near | far | coach | car | taxi | trip

Hi Simon!

It's great that you are coming to my new house next weekend. I know it is a long

¹_____ for you but we will have a great weekend. If you come by ²_____,

get off at the bus stop in the town centre. It's about two miles to my house so get a

³_____ because it's too ⁴_____ to walk with your bag. I'm sorry I can't

pick you up because I haven't got a ⁵_____. I go everywhere here by bicycle. I can

do that because the shops and my college are all ⁶_____ my house.

See you Saturday.

Phil

Exercise 5

Rearrange the letters to find words. Use the definitions to help you.

1 arnit _____ (Get this at a station.)

2 nlaep _____ (Pilots fly this.)

3 ocahc _____ (This is like a bus.)

4 cetitk _____ (You need this on a bus.)

5 odra _____ (Drive your car on this.)

6 yblccei _____ (This usually has two wheels.)

Exercise 6

Have the highlighted words got the correct or incorrect spelling in the sentences?

1 How much was your bus **ticket** ❑?

2 My brother lives **naer** ❑ me.

3 Excuse me, where is the bus **stasion** ❑?

4 I'd like to go by **coatch** ❑ because it's cheaper.

5 How was your **trip** ❑?

6 Does this **trane** ❑ go to Edinburgh?

15

In town

Dear Olga,

Thanks for your letter.

I loved hearing about your life in Russia. I will tell you about the town where I live.

It is a small town and there isn't much to do. We don't have a **cinema** and there is only one **restaurant**.

There are two other girls the same age as me in the **street** where I live, so we often go out together. If the weather is nice, we go to the **park**.

Write again soon!
Kirsty
x

Dear Annette and John,

I'm so pleased you're coming to visit us at last! I'm sure you'll enjoy our lovely **city**!

There are lots of interesting **museums**, and on Sundays there is a really big **market** where you can buy all sorts of things.

Our **flat** is about two miles from the city centre, but there is a **bus stop** at the end of the **road**, so it's easy to get there.
See you soon! We'll come and meet you at the **airport**, of course!

Lots of love
Sara and Rob
xx

To: Brigitte Strauss
From: Emily Mott
Subject: Cambridge meeting

Dear Brigitte

We are very pleased that you are coming to the meeting at our office in Cambridge.

Doug told me that you are arriving at Heathrow **airport** the evening before. There is a **bus station** next to the airport, and you can get a direct bus to Cambridge, but if you prefer to hire a car, there is a **car park** at the **hotel**.

If you click on the link below, you will find a **map** to show you how to get there by car.

Have a good journey!
Emily

> ### Good to know!
>
> A _library_ is a place where you borrow books. You do not have to pay.
> The place where you buy books is called a _book shop_.

Words for talking about towns

airport	NOUN An **airport** is a place where planes come to and go from.
bank	NOUN A **bank** is a place where people can keep their money.
book shop	NOUN A **book shop** is a place that sells books.
bus station	NOUN A **bus station** is a place where buses come to and go from.
bus stop	NOUN A **bus stop** is a place where you can get on a bus.
café	NOUN A **café** is a place where you can buy drinks and small meals.
car park	NOUN A **car park** is an area of ground or a building where people can leave their cars for a period of time.
cinema	NOUN A **cinema** is a building where people watch movies.
city	NOUN A **city** is a large town.
flat	NOUN A **flat** is a set of rooms for living in, usually on one floor.
hotel	NOUN A **hotel** is a building where people pay to sleep and eat meals.
library	NOUN A **library** is a building where books are kept for people to borrow.
map	NOUN A **map** is a drawing of a particular area such as a city or a country, that shows things like mountains, rivers, and roads.
market	NOUN A **market** is a place where people buy and sell products.
museum	NOUN A **museum** is a building where you can look at interesting and valuable objects.
park	NOUN A **park** is a public area of land with grass and trees, usually in a town, where people go to relax and enjoy themselves.
restaurant	NOUN A **restaurant** is a place where you can buy and eat a meal.
road	NOUN A **road** is a long piece of hard ground that vehicles travel on.
school	NOUN A **school** is a place where children go to learn.
shop	NOUN A **shop** is a place that sells things.
street	NOUN A **street** is a road in a city or a town.
town	NOUN A **town** is a place with many streets and buildings where people live and work.

Word Finder

Exercise 1

Match the words with the pictures.

1 map

a

2 park

b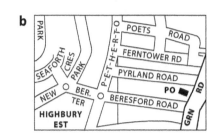

3 restaurant

c

4 shop

d

5 library

e

6 museum

f

Exercise 2

Put the correct word in each gap.

| road | airport | library | café | bank | school | market |

1 Get on a plane here. _____

2 Go out with friends for a coffee here. _____

3 Keep your money here. _____

4 Drive a car on here. _____

5 Buy fruit here. _____

6 Go to lessons in classrooms here. _____

Exercise 3

Rearrange the letters to find words. Use the definitions to help you.

1 stranuarte _____ (Go here to have something to eat.)

2 brilayr _____ (Go here to read books.)

3 sbu psto _____ (Wait here for a bus.)

4 thelo _____ (Sleep here for a few nights.)

5 acr krap _____ (Put your car here.)

6 dora _____ (Cars drive here.)

Exercise 4

Put the correct word in each gap.

| cinema | hotels | street | station | flat | café |

I live in a ¹_____ in an old building. It is opposite two of the city's most famous,

expensive ²_____. I work in a bank, and I always go to work by bus. I catch it at

the bus ³_____ at the end of my ⁴_____. I often have a drink at the

⁵_____ there. After work, I sometimes go to the ⁶_____ to see a film.

Exercise 5

Match the sentence halves.

1 Jack lives

2 I often go to the museum

3 Lots of cars

4 This shop

5 You can get good meals

6 Look at the map

a to look at old pictures.

b in a big new flat.

c in that restaurant.

d sells everything.

e use this road.

f to find the right street.

Exercise 6

Put each sentence into the correct order.

1 park / walk / the / in / we often / .

_____

2 market / Jill / food at / buys / the / .

_____

3 museum / lots of / old / things / has / the / .

_____

4 Tom's / in / this street / school / is / .

_____

5 good coffee / café / sells / that / .

_____

6 map / you can / our road on / see / this / .

_____

16

Health, medicine and exercise

Telling the doctor what is wrong with you

I feel sick/tired.
My neck/leg/back hurts.
I've got toothache/earache/a cough.
I keep getting earache/headaches.

At the doctor's

Doctor	Good morning. What can I do for you?
Amanda	I keep getting **headaches**.
Doctor	Do you have a **cough**?
Amanda	No, but I feel a bit **sick**.
Doctor	Do you eat well and take plenty of **exercise?**
Amanda	I try to, but I feel too **tired** to do any exercise.
Doctor	I see. And are you drinking plenty of water?
Amanda	No, I never drink water. I prefer coffee.
Doctor	That may be the **problem**. Everyone needs to drink water. You should try to have at least five glasses every day. If you do that, your headaches will probably stop.
Amanda	**OK**, I'll try. Thank you, **Dr** Kennedy.

> **Good to know!**
>
> *In the word <u>cough</u>, 'ou' is said like the 'o' in 'hot', and 'gh' is said like the 'f' in 'fish'.*

Words for talking about health, medicine and exercise

baby	NOUN A **baby** is a very young child.
back	NOUN A person's or anilmal's **back** is the part of their body between their head and their legs.
body	NOUN A person's or animal's **body** is all their physical parts.
cold	NOUN If you have a **cold**, you have an illness that makes liquid flow from your nose, and makes you cough.
cough	NOUN A **cough** is an illness in which you suddenly force air out of your throat with a noise.
cut	VERB If you **cut** yourself, you accidentally injure yourself on a sharp object so that you bleed.
doctor	NOUN A **doctor** is a person whose job is to treat people who are sick or injured.
Dr	NOUN **Dr** is the title that goes before the name of a doctor.
earache	NOUN If you have **earache**, you have a pain inside your ear.
exercise	NOUN **Exercise** is movements you do to keep your body healthy and strong.
headache	NOUN If you have a **headache**, you have a pain in your head.
health	NOUN Your **health** is the condition of your body and the extent to which you are fit and well.
hear	VERB When you **hear** a sound, you become aware of it through your ears.
hospital	NOUN A **hospital** is a place where doctors and nurses care for people who are sick or injured.
hurt	VERB If you **hurt** someone or something, you make them feel pain, and if a part of your body hurts, you feel pain there.
leg	NOUN A person's or animal's **legs** are the long parts of their body that they use to stand on.
medicine	NOUN **Medicine** is the treatment of illness and injuries by doctors and nurses.
neck	NOUN Your **neck** is the part of your body between your head and the rest of your body.
nurse	NOUN A **nurse** is a person whose job is to care for people who are sick.
problem	NOUN A **problem** is something that causes difficulties, or that makes you worry.
sick	1 ADJECTIVE If you are **sick**, you are ill. 2 ADJECTIVE If you feel **sick**, you feel as though food might come up from your stomach.
tired	ADJECTIVE If you are **tired**, you feel that you want to rest or sleep.
tooth	NOUN Your teeth are the hard white objects in your mouth, that you use for biting and eating. One of these is called a **tooth**.
toothache	NOUN If you have **toothache**, you have a pain in your tooth.

Exercise 1

Rearrange the letters to find words. Use the definitions to help you.

1 ecrisexe _____ (go running, for example)

2 lopshiat _____ (the place to go when you are sick)

3 besiab _____ (very small people)

4 dybo _____ (swimming is good for your _____)

5 snuer _____ (this person helps you when you are sick)

6 ahre _____ (when you have earache, you sometimes can't do this)

Exercise 2

Match the sentences with the pictures.

1 I've got toothache.

a

2 I've got earache.

b

3 I've got a cough.

c

4 I've got a headache.

d

5 I've got a cold.

e

6 I've got a new baby!

f

Exercise 3

For each question, tick the correct answer.

1 If I study for a long time I get a
- ❏ headache.
- ❏ neck.

2 When you go out in the rain, you can get
- ❏ tired.
- ❏ a cold.

3 See the doctor when you have a
- ❏ problem.
- ❏ tired.

4 I've hurt my
- ❏ earache.
- ❏ neck.

5 I can't go out because I am
- ❏ sick.
- ❏ toothache.

6 Today, I want to do some
- ❏ exercise.
- ❏ cough.

Exercise 4

Match the two parts.

1 My teeth hurt. I've got	**a** earache.
2 I'm coughing a lot. I've got	**b** tired.
3 Dr Thorne works very hard. She often feels	**c** sick.
4 I've cut my arm. I want to see	**d** toothache.
5 I ate something bad. I feel	**e** a cold.
6 That music was very loud. I've got	**f** a doctor.

Exercise 5

Find the words that do not belong, as shown.

1 doctor	nurse	cough
2 baby	cold	headache
3 sick	exercise	tired
4 problem	neck	tooth
5 cough	toothache	hear
6 hospital	cut	hurt

Exercise 6

Put the correct word or words in each gap, as shown.

neck | nurse | doctor | toothache | sick | exercise | tired | hospital

1 a person _____*nurse*_____ _____*doctor*_____

2 a place _____

3 part of the body _____

4 how you feel _____ _____

5 something you can do _____

6 a problem with your teeth _____

17

Food

Types of food

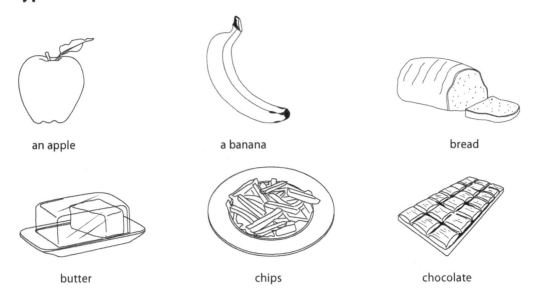

an apple   a banana   bread

butter   chips   chocolate

Talking about food and drink

The following words for types of food and drink are usually uncountable. You cannot put **a** or **an** in front of them. You often put **some** or **any** in front of them.

bread   butter   cheese   chocolate   coffee   meat   milk   fish   fruit   rice

*Would you like **some** bread?*
I usually have coffee with my breakfast.
*We haven't got **any** milk.*
Do you like chocolate?

You can talk about **a piece of bread/chocolate/meat, etc., a cup of coffee** or **a glass/bottle of milk.**

The following words for types of food are usually countable, and you need to use *a* or *an* in front of them. If you put **some** or **any** in front of them, you need to make them plural.

apple   banana   egg

*I took **an** apple to eat after school.*
*I bought **some** bananas.*
*Are there **any** eggs in the fridge?*

The following words for types of food are usually plural.

chips   vegetables

I had meat and vegetables for dinner.
Do you like chips?

Good to know!

Cake can be countable or uncountable.

I bought some cakes for us.

Donna made me a birthday cake.

I ate a lot of cake this afternoon.

Would you like a piece of cake?

Words for talking about food

apple	NOUN	An **apple** is a firm round fruit with green, red, or yellow skin.
banana	NOUN	**Bananas** are long curved fruit with yellow skins.
bread	NOUN	**Bread** is a food made mostly from flour and water.
breakfast	NOUN	**Breakfast** is the first meal of the day, usually eaten in the morning.
butter	NOUN	**Butter** is a soft yellow food made from cream that you put on bread.
cake	NOUN	A **cake** is a sweet food that you make from flour, eggs, sugar, and butter.
cheese	NOUN	**Cheese** is a solid, usually white or yellow, food made from milk.
chips	PLURAL NOUN	**Chips** are long, thin pieces of fried potato.
chocolate	NOUN	**Chocolate** is a sweet brown food that you eat as a sweet.
coffee	NOUN	**Coffee** is a drink made from boiling water and coffee beans.
dinner	NOUN	**Dinner** is the main meal of the day, usually eaten in the evening.
drink	VERB	When you **drink** a liquid, you take it into your mouth and swallow it.
eat	VERB	When you **eat** something, you put it into your mouth and swallow it.
egg	NOUN	An **egg** is a round object that is produced by a female bird, that people eat as food.
fish	NOUN	A **fish** is an animal that lives and swims in water, that people eat as food.
food	NOUN	**Food** is what people and animals eat.
fruit	NOUN	**Fruit** is the part of a tree that contains seeds, covered with a substance that you can eat.
lunch	NOUN	**Lunch** is the meal that you have in the middle of the day.
meat	NOUN	**Meat** is the part of an animal that people cook and eat.
milk	NOUN	**Milk** is the white liquid that cows, and some other animals produce, which people drink.
rice	NOUN	**Rice** is white or brown grains from a plant that grows in wet areas.
vegetables	PLURAL NOUN	**Vegetables** are plants such as carrots, cabbages, and peas.

Word Finder

Exercise 1

Match the words with the pictures.

1 fish

a

2 cake

b

3 banana

c

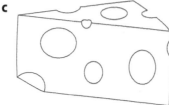

4 egg

d

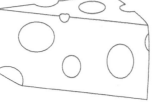

5 cheese

e

6 meat

f

Exercise 2

Rearrange the letters to find words. Use the definitions to help you.

1 uhlnc _____ (We eat this in the middle of the day.)

2 foecef _____ (This is a hot brown drink many people like.)

3 lepaps _____ (These are red and green and grow on trees.)

4 rettbu _____ (It's yellow and we can put it on bread.)

5 getabevels _____ (These are usually green, sometimes red or other colours.)

6 taoloecch _____ (This is sweet and brown and many people like it very much.)

Exercise 3

Match the sentence halves.

1	Many English people	**a**	for dinner this evening?
2	My sister doesn't eat	**b**	cup of coffee?
3	Would you like a	**c**	plenty of water in this hot weather.
4	I had some soup	**d**	like fish and chips.
5	What are you having	**e**	meat or fish.
6	It's good to drink	**f**	and a piece of bread.

Exercise 4

Put each sentence into the correct order.

1 have rice / we usually / for dinner / and vegetables / .

_____

2 I took some / for my lunch / bread and cheese / .

_____

3 good fruit / you can buy / the market / and vegetables at / .

_____

4 dinner / eat chocolate / after / I often / .

_____

5 my salad / I had a / chips with / plate of / .

_____

6 I always / with my / have coffee / breakfast / .

_____

Exercise 5

Choose the correct word or words.

1 I would like **a cheese / some cheese** with my bread.

2 I usually have **meat / a meat** for dinner.

3 My friend made me **cake / a cake** for my birthday.

4 I will take **banana / a banana** to eat later.

5 We are having **fish / a fish** for lunch.

6 I like to eat **a fruit / fruit** every day.

Exercise 6

Complete the sentences by writing one word in each gap.

| eats | drinks | lunch | fruit | cake | milk | fish |

1 Apples and bananas are _____.

2 Lee often _____ rice with his dinner.

3 Ella had eggs for _____.

4 Do you like _____ in your coffee?

5 My mum made me a birthday _____.

6 Paul usually _____ water with his meals.

18

Talking about what you like

We really **enjoyed** our holiday. The weather was **hot** and our hotel was **lovely**. We had **fun** on the beach, and the cities were **great** too.

I never **want** to go on holiday with Peter again! He knows I don't **like** walking, but he made me go up and down mountains all day! I was **hungry** and **thirsty** all the time, and when we got back to our hotel, I was too **tired** to do anything except sleep!

I went out with Lara last night. I wanted to go to an Indian restaurant, but she **prefers** pizza. It was **great** to see her, and we had a really **nice** time. She told me about her new job. She's very **happy** there. I'**d like** to get a new job too.

It is important to use the right verb patterns. When we use another verb after **enjoy**, **like** or **love**, we often use -*ing* forms:

*I enjoy **playing** football.*
*I like **watching** movies.*
*I love **going** on holiday.*

When we use another verb after **prefer**, we use -*ing* forms or **to** + *infinitive*:

*I prefer **playing** tennis.*
*I prefer **to eat** a bit later.*

When we use another verb after **want**, we use **to** + *infinitive*:

*I want **to talk** to Max.*

Words for talking about what you like

cold	ADJECTIVE If something or someone is **cold**, they are not warm.
dislike	VERB If you **dislike** someone or something, you consider them to be unpleasant and do not like them.
enjoy	VERB If you **enjoy** something, you like doing it.
fun	NOUN **Fun** is pleasure and enjoyment.
good	ADJECTIVE **Good** means pleasant or enjoyable.
great	ADJECTIVE If something is **great**, it is very good.
happy	ADJECTIVE Someone who is **happy** feels pleased and satisfied.
hope	VERB If you **hope** that something is true, or that something will happen, you want it to be true or you want it to happen.
hot	1 ADJECTIVE Something that is **hot** has a high temperature. 2 ADJECTIVE If someone is **hot**, they feel uncomfortable because the temperature is too high.
hungry	ADJECTIVE When you are **hungry**, you want to eat.
interesting	ADJECTIVE If something is **interesting**, it keeps your attention.
like	VERB If you **like** someone or something, you think they are interesting, enjoyable or attractive.
love	VERB If you **love** something, you like it very much.
lovely	ADJECTIVE If someone or something is **lovely**, they are beautiful, very nice, or very enjoyable.
nice	ADJECTIVE If something is **nice**, it is attractive, pleasant, or enjoyable.
prefer	VERB If you **prefer** someone or something, you like that person or thing better than another.
sad	ADJECTIVE If you are **sad**, you feel unhappy.
thirsty	ADJECTIVE If you are **thirsty**, you want to drink something.
tired	ADJECTIVE If you are **tired**, you feel that you want to rest or sleep.
want	VERB If you **want** something, you feel a need for it.
would like	PHRASE If you say that you **would like** something or **would like** to do something, you are indicating a wish or desire that you have.

Word Finder

Exercise 1

Match the two parts.

1 Mark would like a drink. He's   a tired.

2 I need a thick sweater. This room is   b cold.

3 Don't touch the oven door. It's very   c thirsty.

4 Jenny wants an apple. She's   d hot.

5 He worked late last night. He's really   e hungry.

Exercise 2

Put the correct word in each gap.

| want | fun | hope | prefer | enjoy | like |

Hi Lucy

Would you ¹_____ to come to the fair with me tomorrow? Do you
²_____ the morning or afternoon? I ³_____ to go in the afternoon, at
about 3 p.m. I think we can have ⁴_____ there. I ⁵_____ everything at
the fair. I ⁶_____ you can come with me.

Love

Sam

Exercise 3

Which sentences are correct?

1 I worked hard yesterday, so I tired today.   ❏

2 That's a great jacket and it's a lovely colour.   ❏

3 Our hotel was nice and the weather wasn't very hot.   ❏

4 My sister's sad, because her friend is very ill.   ❏

5 Are you interesting in this book?   ❏

6 The film was fun nice and we laughed a lot.   ❏

Exercise 4

Are the highlighted words correct or incorrect in the sentences?

1 I want to find an **interesting** ❏ job when I leave school.

2 Malik is always very hot and **thirsty** ❏ after a football match.

3 There's coffee or tea. Which do you **love** ❏?

4 Lee doesn't **like** ❏ to come out with us because he's tired.

5 Did you have a **good** ❏ time at the party?

6 Would you **enjoy** ❏ to have lunch with me tomorrow?

Exercise 5

Match the words with the pictures.

1 happy

2 hungry

3 cold

4 thirsty

5 hot

6 sad

Exercise 6

Rearrange the letters to find words. Use the definitions to help you.

1 istryth _____ (you want a drink)

2 gesterinint _____ (a way to describe a good story)

3 volley _____ (beautiful or nice)

4 gater _____ (very good)

5 rughyn _____ (you need to eat something)

6 driet _____ (you'd like to sit down)

19

Travel and holidays

Visiting my aunt

I went to the station by bicycle.

I bought a ticket to Bristol.

I got there at 9.30 and my aunt met me.

She drove me to her house.

A holiday in Australia

I flew to Brisbane.

After a few days, I went by boat to one of the beautiful islands.

I went swimming every day. It was fantastic!

I was sad when it was time to leave.

Words for talking about travel and holidays

bicycle	NOUN A **bicycle** is a vehicle with two wheels which you ride by sitting on it and using your legs to make the wheels turn.
boat	NOUN A **boat** is a small ship.
bus	NOUN A **bus** is a large motor vehicle that carries passengers.
car	NOUN A **car** is a motor vehicle with space for about five people.
drive	VERB When you **drive**, you control the movement and direction of a car or other vehicle.
driver	NOUN A **driver** is the person who drives a car.
fly	VERB If you **fly** somewhere, you travel there in an aircraft.

Word Finder

holiday	NOUN A **holiday** is a period of time when you relax and enjoy yourself away from home.
hotel	NOUN A **hotel** is a building where people pay to sleep and eat meals.
leave	VERB If you **leave** a place or a person, you go away from them.
plane	NOUN A **plane** is a vehicle with wings and engines that can fly.
station	NOUN A **station** is a place where trains stop so that people can get on or off.
taxi	NOUN A **taxi** is a car with its driver, who you pay to take you where you want to go.
ticket	NOUN A **ticket** is a small piece of paper that shows that you have paid to go somewhere or to do something.
train	NOUN A **train** is a long vehicle that is pulled by an engine along a railway.
travel	VERB If you **travel**, you go from one place to another, often to a place that is far away.
visit	VERB If you **visit** someone, you go to see them in order to spend time with them.

Exercise 1

Put the correct word in each gap.

hotels | holiday | taxi | leaves | ticket | visit | travel

Hi Mike

I'm going on holiday to Scotland next week. I'm going to ¹_____ my friend Tom, and I can stay in his house. That's good because ²_____ there are very expensive. I don't want to ³_____ there by car because it's so far and my car is very old. So yesterday I bought a ⁴_____ for a very early train next Monday morning. I will get a ⁵_____ to the station at 5 a.m. because my train ⁶_____ at 5.45.

Talk to you soon,

Chris

Exercise 2

Are the highlighted words correct or incorrect in the sentences?

1 I'm going to France **by** ❑ plane.
2 My hotel is near the beach and I **get** ❑ swimming every day.
3 He's a very good **driver** ❑.
4 **Go** ❑ the number 10 bus from outside the bank.
5 Can you **get** ❑ a train from the city centre to your village?
6 Does your bus **visit** ❑ at 9.30 or 9.20?

Exercise 3

Complete the sentences by writing one word in each gap.

1 Do you travel _____ bus when you go on holiday?

2 Let's go _____ Paris this weekend. I want to see the Eiffel Tower!

3 She _____ her car very fast.

4 I'm going to meet Sarah at the railway _____ at 2.30.

5 Yesterday, we _____ the museum and saw some interesting old photos there.

6 Everyone must buy a train _____ before they get on the train.

Exercise 4

Choose the correct word.

1 How did you **travel / stay / visit** to the mountains?

2 Why do you want to go there **on / by / in** bus?

3 What time does your train **travel / drive / leave**?

4 Can I **go / get / travel** a bus to the sports centre from here?

5 There is a very interesting museum you can **stay / go / visit** in town.

6 We went to the seaside and went fishing in a **boat / car / bus**.

Exercise 5

Which sentences are correct?

1 The taxi drive is waiting for us in the hotel lobby. ❏

2 He couldn't get a bus because it was late at night. ❏

3 The hotels has a fantastic swimming pool. ❏

4 I don't like flying because it's uncomfortable. ❏

5 Where are you getting on holiday this year? ❏

6 Will you visit to your aunt when you go to San Francisco? ❏

20

Weather

Bad weather

It was dangerous to drive because it was so foggy.

In winter, there is often ice on the road.

It was too wet to go out, so I had to wait for the rain to stop.

It was difficult to ride my bicycle because it was so windy.

Good weather

The sky was blue with a few white clouds.

We had a lovely sunny day for our wedding.

We had dinner outside because the weather was so warm.

We had a very hot summer this year.

Good to know!

Several adjectives that describe weather are formed with the suffix -y.

cloud > cloudy

fog > foggy

sun > sunny

wind > windy

Words for talking about weather

cloud	NOUN A **cloud** is a white or grey mass in the sky that contains drops of water.
cloudy	ADJECTIVE If it is **cloudy**, there are a lot of clouds in the sky.
cold	ADJECTIVE **Cold** describes the weather when the temperature is low.
fog	NOUN **Fog** is thick cloud that is close to the ground.
foggy	ADJECTIVE When it is **foggy**, there is fog.
hot	ADJECTIVE **Hot** describes the weather when the temperature is high.
ice	NOUN **Ice** is frozen water.
rain	NOUN **Rain** is water that falls from the clouds in small drops.
sky	NOUN The **sky** is the space above the Earth that you can see when you stand outside and look up.
snow	NOUN **Snow** is soft white frozen water that falls from the sky.
summer	NOUN **Summer** is the season between spring and autumn.
sun	NOUN The **sun** is the ball of fire in the sky that gives us heat and light.
sunny	ADJECTIVE When it is **sunny**, the sun shines brightly.
warm	ADJECTIVE Something that is **warm** has some heat, but is not hot.
weather	NOUN The **weather** is the temperature and conditions outside, for example if it is raining, hot, or windy.
wet	ADJECTIVE If the weather is **wet**, it is raining.
wind	NOUN **Wind** is air that moves.
windy	ADJECTIVE If it is **windy**, the wind is blowing a lot.
winter	NOUN **Winter** is the season between autumn and spring.

Exercise 1

Decide if the pairs of sentences have the same meaning.

1 **A** Yesterday it was sunny.
    B Yesterday the sun was shining.

2 **A** It was cold last night.
    B It wasn't warm last night.

3 **A** There is ice on the road so it is difficult to drive on.
    B The road is closed because the weather is very bad.

4 **A** There are lots of clouds in the sky.
    B It is raining at the moment.

5 **A** It's warm so you don't need a sweater.
    B You need more clothes in this weather.

6 **A** It's hot here in summer.
    B The summer weather is very warm in this place.

Exercise 2

Match the words with the pictures.

1 cloudy

2 windy

3 rain

4 sunny

5 foggy

6 snow

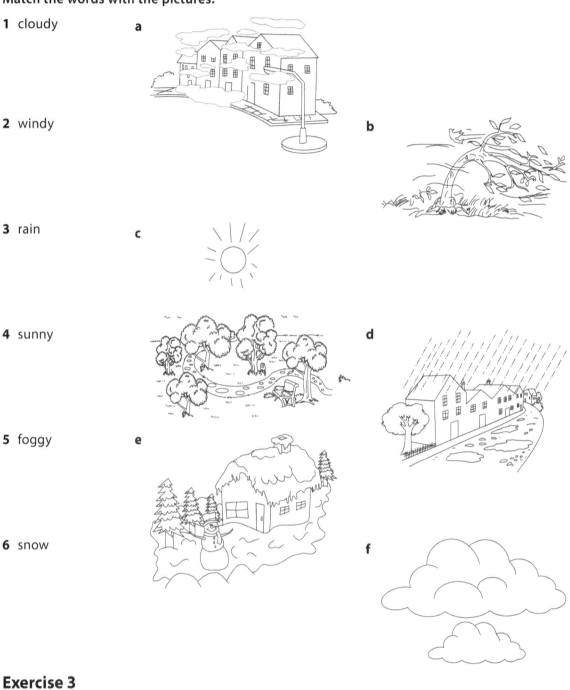

Exercise 3

Put the correct word in each gap.

| snow | summer | rains | cloudy | sky | sunny |

The weather in Scotland changes a lot. In winter there is ¹_____ on the mountains and you can go skiing. Sometimes the ²_____ is blue and it's beautiful but sometimes it's ³_____. You need warm clothes in winter and it ⁴_____ a lot, so you need an umbrella. In ⁵_____ it is often warm and ⁶_____, so it is a good time to go there for a holiday.

Exercise 4

Rearrange the letters to find words. Use the definitions to help you.

1 cei _____ (It's dangerous to drive when this is on the road.)

2 ygogf _____ (It's difficult to see in this kind of weather.)

3 nidwy _____ (It's difficult to use an umbrella in this kind of weather.)

4 olucd _____ (This is a white or grey thing in the sky.)

5 mumser _____ (It is hotter than the other times of the year.)

6 nwos _____ (This is white and cold and falls from the sky.)

Exercise 5

Are the highlighted words correct or incorrect in this text?

My summer holiday blog

It's Monday and I'm still on holiday in France. There isn't a **cloud** ❏ in the sky. I'm sure it will be **sun** ❏ today and we can go to the beach. I want to go sailing but if it is too **wind** ❏, we can't go because it's dangerous. It's the same problem if it's **fog** ❏. Yesterday it wasn't very **hot** ❏ but it was OK. At home in Canada it's **raining** ❏ at the moment, so I'm glad I'm on holiday here.

Exercise 6

Choose the correct word.

1 There's a big white **wind / rain / cloud** in the sky.

2 Oh no! It's raining so we will get **warm / wet / hot**.

3 The **weather / sky / cloud** was warm when we were on holiday.

4 I like **wind / winter / summer** because I can go skiing then.

5 It was **cold / foggy / sunny** yesterday so we went to the beach.

6 I can't see the top of the mountains because there's a lot of **weather / sky / fog**.

21

Natural world

Dear Martha

You asked me to tell you about where I live. Our house is next to a large **forest**, where we can go walking and climb in the **trees**. Behind the forest, there are mountains. They are so high that they have **snow** on them, even in **summer**.

Our house is nearly 15 miles from the nearest town. I love living in the **country**, but if you come to visit, it will be strange for you to be so far away from a city.

Write soon!
Liesl

a forest

a beach and the sea

Dear Liesl

Thank you for telling me about the **place** where you live! It sounds very different from my home! I live in a big city. It is a beautiful city, with a **river** running through the middle of it.

We have a small garden and my mum likes to grow lots of **flowers**. The city also has lots of parks with nice **plants** in them.

When the **weather** is **hot**, we go to the **beach**. It only takes half an hour in the car.

Your friend
Martha

Words for talking about the natural world

Word Finder

beach	NOUN A **beach** is an area of sand or stones next to a lake or the sea.
cold	ADJECTIVE **Cold** describes the weather when the temperature is low.
country	1 NOUN A **country** is an area of the world with its own government and people. 2 NOUN The **country** is land that is away from cities and towns.
flower	NOUN A **flower** is the brightly coloured part of a plant.
forest	NOUN A **forest** is a large area where trees grow close together.
grass	NOUN **Grass** is a plant with thin, green leaves that cover the surface of the ground.
hot	ADJECTIVE **Hot** describes the weather when the temperature is high.
place	NOUN A **place** is a particular building, area, town, or country.
plant	NOUN A **plant** is a living thing that grows in the earth and has a stem, leaves, and roots.
rain	1 NOUN **Rain** is water that falls from the clouds in small drops. 2 VERB When **rain** falls, you can say that it is raining.
river	NOUN A **river** is a long line of water that flows into the sea.
sea	NOUN The **sea** is a large area of salty water.
snow	NOUN **Snow** is soft white frozen water that falls from the sky.
summer	NOUN **Summer** is the season between spring and autumn and is usually the hottest part of the year.
sun	NOUN The **sun** is the ball of fire in the sky that gives us heat and light.
tree	NOUN A **tree** is a tall plant with a hard central part (= a trunk), branches, and leaves.
warm	ADJECTIVE Something that is **warm** has some heat, but is not hot.
weather	NOUN The **weather** is the temperature and conditions outside, for example if it is raining, hot, or windy.
winter	NOUN **Winter** is the season between autumn and spring and is usually the coldest part of the year.
world	NOUN The **world** is the planet that we live on.

Exercise 1

Rearrange the letters to find words. Use the definitions to help you.

1 habec _____ (a place by the sea)

2 ostref _____ (lots of trees)

3 rewolf _____ (a beautiful part of a plant)

4 mermus _____ (the warm time of the year)

5 thawree _____ (this can change every day in England)

6 drowl _____ (we all live in this)

Exercise 2

Match the words with the pictures.

1 sun

a

2 snow

b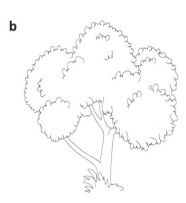

3 grass

c

4 plant

d

5 rain

e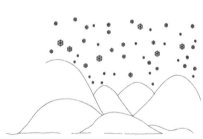

6 tree

f

Exercise 3

Find the words that do not belong, as shown.

1 Describing weather	warm	cold	sun
2 Things in a garden	forest	plant	flower
3 Water	sea	tree	river
4 Places	country	beach	grass
5 Seasons	snow	winter	summer

Exercise 4

Choose the correct word.

1 I feel happy when the **hot / sun / summer** is shining.

2 We often go for a walk in the **forest / trees / grass** at the weekend.

3 There is usually **flower / cold / snow** here in the winter.

4 People don't stay on the beach when it **rains / plants / rivers**.

5 Did you have good **warm / place / weather** for your birthday party?

Exercise 5

Are the highlighted words correct or incorrect in the sentences?

1 What kind of weather do you have in your part of the **world** ☐?

2 That plant has very nice **trees** ☐ and flowers.

3 I enjoy walking in the **weather** ☐.

4 The sea is **warm** ☐ in the summer, so we can swim in it.

5 We wanted to go out, but it began to **rain** ☐.

6 We never see snow in my country, because it's very **summer** ☐.

Exercise 6

Put the correct word in each gap.

| summer | flower | forest | sea | river | tree | beach |

The ¹_____ begins in a beautiful ²_____ under a tall, old

³_____. Then it goes through a town and comes to the ⁴_____. There is

a small ⁵_____ where people can enjoy the warm sun in ⁶_____.

22

Entertainment and the media

Music

I am a music teacher, but I'm also in a **band**. I play the **guitar** and my friend **sings**. Jazz is the kind of **music** we like best.

Good to know!

You say that someone plays <u>in</u> a group or a band, and that people listen <u>to</u> music.

Free time

I go to the **cinema** every week. I love watching old **movies**!

My husband and I love **dancing**! We usually go to a **dance** on Saturday evenings.

I am learning to **paint**. My **pictures** aren't very good yet!

Newspapers, radio and television

It is important to use the right prepositions:

*I listened to a show **on** the radio.*
*I like listening **to** the radio.*
*I read it **in** the newspaper.*
*I saw it **on** the television.*

Words for talking about entertainment and the media

band	NOUN A **band** is a group of people who play music together.
book	NOUN A **book** is a number of pieces of paper, usually with words printed on them, that are fastened together and fixed inside a cover.
camera	NOUN A **camera** is a piece of equipment for taking photographs or making movies.
cinema	NOUN A **cinema** is a building where people go to watch movies.
dance	1 VERB When you **dance**, you move your body to music. 2 NOUN A **dance** is a particular series of movements that you usually do to music.
dancing	NOUN **Dancing** is when people dance.
draw	VERB When you **draw**, you use a pencil or pen to make a picture.
entertainment	NOUN **Entertainment** consists of performances or activities that give people pleasure.
film	NOUN A **film** is a movie.
group	NOUN A **group** is a number of people who play music together.
guitar	NOUN A **guitar** is a musical instrument with strings.
media	NOUN You can refer to television, radio, and newspapers as **the media**.
movie	NOUN A **movie** is a story that is shown in a series of moving pictures.
music	NOUN **Music** is the pleasant sound that you make when you sing or play instruments.
newspaper	NOUN A **newspaper** is a number of large sheets of folded paper, with news, advertisements, and other information printed on them.
page	NOUN A **page** is one side of a piece of paper in a book, a magazine, or a newspaper.
paint	VERB If you **paint** something or paint a picture of it, you produce a picture of it using paint.
photo	NOUN A **photo** is a picture made with a camera.
picture	NOUN A **picture** is a drawing, painting or photograph.
radio	NOUN A **radio** is a piece of equipment that you use in order to listen to radio programmes.
sing	VERB When you **sing**, you make music with your voice.
television/TV	NOUN A **television** or a **TV** is a piece of electrical equipment with a screen on which you watch moving pictures with sound.

Exercise 1

Put the correct word in each gap.

| films | radio | cinemas | music | group | sang | guitar |

The Beatles – John, Paul, George and Ringo – were a famous pop [1]_____ of the 1960s. Ringo played the drums, the other three played the [2]_____ and they all [3]_____. Their records were on the [4]_____ all the time. They also made several [5]_____. These were shown in [6]_____ all over the world and were very popular.

Exercise 2

Match the words with the pictures.

1 camera

2 newspaper

3 photo

4 television

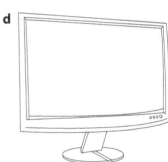

5 guitar

6 book

Exercise 3

Which sentences are correct?

1 In the 1977 film Saturday Night Fever, John Travolta played someone who loved dancing. ❏

2 The artist Pablo Picasso painted a lot of pictures and people can see them on the radio. ❏

3 In the past you needed a camera to take books, but now you can take them with a mobile phone. ❏

4 Shall we go to the radio and watch a movie? ❏

5 The Twist was a popular dance of the 1960s. ❏

6 There's an interesting picture on page 6 of the newspaper. ❏

Exercise 4

Are the highlighted words correct or incorrect in the sentences?

1 I like listening to **music** ❏ played on the guitar.

2 I enjoy watching **cinemas** ❏ that make me laugh.

3 I like **drawing** ❏, but I'm better at painting.

4 I learned to play the **band** ❏ when I was a child.

5 My parents gave me an expensive **camera** ❏, so now I can take good photos.

6 I enjoy listening to Frances, as she **sings** ❏ very well.

Exercise 5

Choose the correct word.

1 The teacher asked the children to draw a **film / music / picture** of their family.

2 I often listen to classical music on the **radio / movie / book**.

3 How many **pages / groups / dances** of sport are there in your newspaper?

4 A **camera / cinema / band** played the music at Toby and Jill's wedding.

5 This book has hundreds of **newspapers / photos / paints** of animals.

Exercise 6

Match the sentence halves.

1 Would you like to go to the cinema	**a**	and some of her pictures are very good.
2 The school started a band	**b**	and see a comedy film?
3 Eleanor likes drawing	**c**	so children could play music together.
4 Jane and Darrell like music	**d**	or do you usually watch it on TV?
5 My friend George can sing	**e**	and they go dancing every week.
6 Do you listen to the news on the radio	**f**	and play the guitar.

23

Phrases with *do, get, go, have, make* and *take*

Do and Make

These are some common ways to use **do** and **make**:

do + activity	*I have to **do** my homework.* *We **did** exercise 6 from our English book.*
make + food	*He **made** a cake for me.* *I often **make** bread.*

Get

These are some common ways to use **get**:

get = receive	*He **got** lots of presents.*
get = buy	*I **got** a new coat.*
get = arrive	*We **got** home late.*
get = travel	*Let's **get** the bus.* *We **got** a train to London.*
get up = get out of bed	*What time do you **get up**?*

Go

These are some common ways to use **go**:

go + activity	*Shall we **go** swimming?*
go by + vehicle	*We **went by** bus.* *He usually **goes by** car.*
go to + place	*She **went** to China.* *I want to **go to** the theatre.*
go for + activity	*Let's **go for** a walk.*

Have

These are some common ways to use **have**:

have + description of a body part	*He **has** blue eyes.* *She **has** very long legs.*
have + illness	*He **had** a cold.* *She **had** a headache.*
have + food or drink	*Let's **have** a cup of tea.* *He **had** pizza for lunch.*
have + action	*I need to **have** a shower.*
have + holiday	*We **had** a holiday in Wales.* *You need to **have** a holiday.*

Take

These are some common ways to use **take**:

take + object	I **took** my mobile phone. You should **take** an umbrella.
take + person	I **took** the kids to the park. Can you **take** John to his football match?
take + photo	She **took** a photo of the house.
take + activity	I need to **take** a shower.

Exercise 1

Match the sentences with the pictures.

1 He is taking a photo.

2 He is having a drink.

3 He is going for a walk.

4 He is doing his homework.

5 He is making dinner.

6 He is having a shower.

a

b

c

d

e

f

Exercise 2

Choose the correct word.

1 I got up and **made / had** a shower.

2 We **took / had** a really nice holiday.

3 Sam is still asleep. Could you **get / make** him up, please?

4 He usually **makes / gets** home from work at six o'clock.

5 The teacher asked us to **do / make** exercise 6 on page 13.

6 I **got / took** a very special birthday present from my parents.

Exercise 3

Put each sentence into the correct order.

1 eyes / has / father / my / blue / .

_____

2 cold / have / I / a / bad / really / .

_____

3 you / could / get / bread / please / some / ?

_____

4 we / some / food / had / delicious / .

_____

5 got / a / I / bus / restaurant / the / to / .

_____

6 took / me / phone / I / with / my / .

_____

Exercise 4

Write the simple past form of the verb in (brackets) to complete each sentence.

1 My mum _____ (make) some food for us.

2 I _____ (get) a new bike for my birthday.

3 We _____ (go) to Paris by train.

4 I _____ (take) the dog to the park.

5 We _____ (have) a lovely holiday.

6 For homework, I _____ (do) exercises nine and ten.

Exercise 5

Match the sentence halves.

1 Sara made

2 We went

3 I remembered to take

4 I got some

5 Have

6 I did my

a homework when I got home from school.

b to the city centre by taxi.

c lovely presents for my birthday.

d dinner for her family.

e my camera to the party.

f a great holiday!

24

Words that connect sentences

Conjunctions

Conjunctions are words that join two parts of a sentence together:

*I stood up **and** walked to the door.*
*It's cold in here **because** the window is open.*
*I like fish **but** I don't like meat.*
*I saw Paul **when** I was in town.*
*It was raining **so** I took my umbrella.*

Starting sentences

Some adverbs are often used to start sentences, especially when you are speaking:

***Now**, tell me a bit about your family.*
***So**, did you enjoy the show?*
***Well**, I'm not sure, really.*

Good to know!

Be careful to put the word <u>also</u> in the correct place. Usually it comes before the verb:

Tom <u>also bought</u> an ice cream.

However, it comes after the verb <u>be</u>:

My sister was <u>also</u> happy about it.

Connecting words

also	ADVERB You can use **also** to give more information about something.
and	CONJUNCTION You use **and** to connect two or more words or phrases.
because	CONJUNCTION You use **because** when you are giving the reason for something.
but	CONJUNCTION You use **but** to introduce something that is different from what you have just said.
now	ADVERB You use **now** to start talking about something new.
OK	ADJECTIVE You use **OK** to say that you agree with something.
or	CONJUNCTION You use **or** to show choices or possibilities.

Word Finder

Word Finder	**really**	1 ADVERB You can say **'really?'** to express surprise at what someone has said.
		2 ADVERB You use **really** to make what you are saying stronger.
	so	1 CONJUNCTION You use **so** to introduce the result of a situation.
		2 ADVERB You can use **so** in conversations to introduce a new subject.
	then	ADVERB You use **then** to say that one thing happens after another.
	well	ADVERB You use **well** before you begin to speak, or when you are surprised about something.
	when	1 CONJUNCTION You use **when** to introduce the part of the sentence where you mention the time at which something happens.
		2 PRONOUN You use **when** to ask questions about the time at which things happen.

Exercise 1

Match the sentence halves.

1 I'd like to have a pizza

2 The sports centre was closed

3 Don't drink more than two

4 Come and sit down,

5 The film ended

6 Thelma had a party

a but first tell me your name.

b or three cups of coffee a day.

c when the two main people got married.

d so we couldn't go to the gym.

e and some salad, please.

f because it was her birthday.

Exercise 2

Put the correct word in each gap.

also | or | when | because | but | so

Hi Walid!

You should visit Buckingham Palace ¹_____ you go to London. I think you should
²_____ go to the National Gallery, ³_____ you like paintings. Lots of
tourists visit the Tower of London, ⁴_____ you should go there, ⁵_____
it's best to go early, before there are lots of people. Later, you may have to wait an hour
⁶_____ more to get in.

Have a great time in London!

Sue

Exercise 3

Are the highlighted words correct or incorrect in this text?

Good afternoon, ladies **or** ❑ gentlemen. My name's Jeanette, **and** ❑ I'm your guide this
afternoon. **Now** ❑, we're going to visit the city wall, **because** ❑ before we do, I'd like to tell you
something about the history of the city. **So** ❑ when did the first people live here? **Well** ❑, you'll
be surprised how long ago that was.

Exercise 4

Choose the correct word.

1 I like going to the cinema in my free time. I **and / also / but** like playing tennis.

2 **Now / Really / Because** let's talk about your new job.

3 A I'm very famous indeed – everyone knows me.
   B **OK / Really / Then**?

4 **Or / When / Well**, it's very nice to see you again.

5 **Also / So / Because** why did you come to Australia?

6 A I'm sorry I'm late.
   B That's **OK / now / well**.

Exercise 5

Which sentences are correct?

1 Now, do you have any more questions?   ❏

2 When, we've got a lot of things to see.   ❏

3 Charlie Chaplin acted in films and he also wrote music for his films.   ❏

4 Would you prefer to go swimming but to stay at home?   ❏

5 Really, this is the most beautiful city in the world!   ❏

6 So, tell me about your holiday.   ❏

Exercise 6

Put each sentence into the correct order.

1 pleased / here / , / I'm very / well / you're / .

   _____

2 ice cream / , / wants / now / an / who / ?

   _____

3 home / we / when / go / shall / ?

   _____

4 in the / you / can swim / OK / , / river / .

   _____

5 that / know / I didn't / really / ! / ?

   _____

6 you / so / do / from / where / come / ?

   _____

25

Where things are

To: Alex Painter
From: Peter Adams
Subject: Party

Hi Alex!

Really pleased you can come to the party! Our **address** is 47, Bridge Road. If you're coming from the town centre, you need to **go** right just **before** the church. Keep driving **down** that road. Our house is **near** a big tree, **opposite** the post office. You can park **outside** the house.

See you on Saturday!
Peter

Marisa is coming **downstairs**. Her dog is waiting **at** the **bottom** of the stairs.

Max is standing at the **top** of a ladder. His wife is looking **out of** the window to see what he is doing.

Maria is **putting** her clothes in the cupboard. **There are** already a lot of clothes in it.

Words for talking about where things are

address	NOUN Your **address** is the number of the building, the name of the street, and the town or city where you live.
at	PREPOSITION You use **at** to say where something happens or is situated.
before	PREPOSITION If one place is **before** another, it comes first.
below	PREPOSITION If something is **below** something else, it is in a lower position.
bottom	1 ADJECTIVE The **bottom** thing is the lowest one. 2 NOUN The **bottom** of something is the lowest or deepest part of it.
by	PREPOSITION Someone or something that is **by** something else is beside it.
down	PREPOSITION **Down** means toward a lower level, or in a lower place.
downstairs	ADVERB If you go **downstairs** in a building, you walk down the stairs toward the ground floor.
go	VERB When you **go** somewhere, you move or travel there.
map	NOUN A **map** is a drawing of a particular area such as a city or a country, that shows things like mountains, rivers, and roads.
near	PREPOSITION If something is **near** a place, a thing, or a person, it is a short distance from them.
opposite	PREPOSITION If one person or thing is **opposite** another, it is across from them.
out	ADVERB When you take something **out**, you remove it from a place.
out of	PREPOSITION If you take something **out of** a container or place, you remove it.
outside	PREPOSITION If you are **outside** a place, you are not in it.
place	NOUN A **place** is a particular building, area, town, or country.
put	VERB If you **put** something in a particular place or position, you move it into that place or position.
there is/are	PHRASE You use **there is** or **there are** to describe that something exists or is in a certain place.
top	1 ADJECTIVE The **top** thing is the highest one. 2 NOUN The **top** of something is its highest point.
up	PREPOSITION **Up** means towards a higher place.

Word Finder

Exercise 1

Which sentences are correct?

1 My address is at 21 High Street. ❏
2 The bus stop is in near my house. ❏
3 She took the new TV out of the box. ❏
4 Sally ran downstairs to answer the front door. ❏
5 There's a small park opposite of my school. ❏
6 We live in the top flat and can see the sea from our windows. ❏ ❏

Exercise 2

Choose the correct word.

1 Do you know the **place / map / address** of Danny's school?

2 Please leave your wet shoes **out / out of / outside** the door.

3 The bathroom is at the **top / opposite / up** of the stairs.

4 The eggs are on the shelf **below / bottom / down** the milk and cheese.

5 Let's meet **before / by / downstairs** the entrance of the cinema.

Exercise 3

Put the correct word in each gap.

at	near	down	place	opposite	map	out of

When I arrived ¹_____ the airport, I found a ²_____, but the

³_____ I wanted wasn't on it. I asked a woman to help me and she told me it

was very ⁴_____. 'Go ⁵_____ the airport doors and you can see it on

the ⁶_____ side of the road,' she said. It was so easy to find!

Exercise 4

Put each sentence into the correct order.

1 downstairs / get / I / my watch / to / went / .

_____

2 his pocket / of / took / Andy / his key / out / .

_____

3 of / we walked / the hill / the top / to / .

_____

4 the sports centre / the footballer / a photo / below / of / sat / .

_____

5 the house / my phone / can only / outside / I / use / .

_____

6 a café / lunch / her office / at / Kirsten has / opposite / .

_____

Exercise 5

Rearrange the letters to find words. Use the definitions to help you.

1 udetiso _____ (not in the house)

2 robeef _____ (not after)

3 tomtob _____ (not the top)

4 sadders _____ (where you live)

5 stopipeo _____ (on the other side)

6 daswrotins _____ (at the bottom of the stairs)

26

What is it like? How is it done?

Yesterday, I went to see my little sister and her friends doing a concert at their school. I got there **early** so that I could sit at the front. My sister plays the piano, and I was surprised, because I had no idea she was so **good**! Her friend plays the violin, and they played some pieces **together.** The **last** piece was really **difficult**. It was very **fast**, but they played it really **well**.

Last night, Tom and I went to the French restaurant in town for the first **time**. Everything was really **slow**. It took more than an hour to get our food. Tom asked to have his steak without the sauce, and the waiter told him that was not **possible**! The food was very **poor**, and the restaurant didn't look very **clean**. One thing is certain – we'll **never** go there again!

Good to know!

Be careful to use <u>always</u> and <u>never</u> in the right place in a sentence.
They usually come before the verb:
Marie <u>always</u> has eggs for breakfast.
They <u>never</u> talk to me.
However, they come after the verb <u>be</u>:
Hal is <u>always</u> late.
My brother is <u>never</u> home.

always	ADVERB	If you **always** do something, you do it whenever a particular situation happens.
bored	ADJECTIVE	If you are **bored**, you are not interested in something or you have nothing to do.
careful	ADJECTIVE	If you are **careful**, you think a lot about what you are doing so that you do not make any mistakes.
clean	ADJECTIVE	Something that is **clean** is not dirty.
correct	ADJECTIVE	Something is **correct** when it is right or true.
difficult	ADJECTIVE	Something that is **difficult** is not easy to do, understand, or deal with.
early	ADVERB	**Early** means before the usual time or at the beginning of the day.
fast	ADJECTIVE	Something or someone that is **fast** is quick.
first	ADJECTIVE, ADVERB	**First** means coming before all the others.
funny	ADJECTIVE	Someone or something that is **funny** is amusing and likely to make you smile or laugh.
good		1 ADJECTIVE **Good** means pleasant or enjoyable. 2 ADJECTIVE **Good** means of a high quality or level.

Word Finder

	last	1 ADJECTIVE The **last** event, person, or thing is the most recent one.
		2 ADJECTIVE The **last** thing, person, event, or period of time is the one that happens or comes after all the others of the same type.
	never	ADVERB **Never** means at no time in the past, the present, or the future.
	OK	ADJECTIVE If something is **OK**, you are allowed to do it.
	poor	ADJECTIVE Something that is **poor** is bad.
	possible	ADJECTIVE If it is **possible** to do something, that thing can be done.
	quick	ADJECTIVE Something that is **quick** takes or lasts only a short time.
	slow	ADJECTIVE If something is **slow**, it does not move or happen quickly.
	time	NOUN When you talk about a **time** when something happens, you are referring to a specific occasion when it happens.
	together	ADVERB If people do something **together**, they do it with each other.
	well	ADVERB If you do something **well**, you do it in a good way.

Exercise 1

For each question, tick the correct answer.

1 We laugh when something is
 ❑ funny.
 ❑ well.

2 When we have nothing to do, we are
 ❑ correct.
 ❑ bored.

3 We wash things to make them
 ❑ quick.
 ❑ clean.

4 Learning English is sometimes
 ❑ bored.
 ❑ difficult.

5 Living without water is not
 ❑ possible.
 ❑ fast.

6 When we use a knife, we must be
 ❑ slow.
 ❑ careful.

Exercise 2

Match the sentence halves.

1 The food at this restaurant

2 My mother likes

3 The first lesson

4 We always play football

5 Anna and Max went

6 Is it OK to

a to the theatre together.

b to get up early.

c at the weekend.

d today is history.

e is very good.

f open the window?

Exercise 3

Choose the correct word.

1 What is the **difficult / correct** answer?

2 What time is the **clean / fast** train to London?

3 I have a **quick / correct** shower every morning.

4 Bill is usually the **last / correct** person to arrive.

5 The teacher gives us **bored / difficult** work to do.

6 I would like a **clean / last** plate, please.

Exercise 4

Put each sentence into the correct order.

1 never / reads / books / my sister / .

_____

2 very poor / Ivan's / English / is / .

_____

3 the piano / Anna / plays / very well / .

_____

4 together / school / we always / walk to / .

_____

5 a very / is / this / slow train / .

_____

6 OK to take / is / this chair / it / ?

_____

Exercise 5

Put the correct word in each gap.

| last | poor | early | clean | slow | good | difficult |

1 The opposite of dirty is _____ .

2 The opposite of bad is _____ .

3 The opposite of quick is _____ .

4 The opposite of first is _____ .

5 The opposite of easy is _____ .

6 The opposite of late is _____ .

Exercise 6

Put the correct word in each gap.

| together | possible | bored | funny | good | always |

When the weather is [1]_____, my friend Alex and I often go to the beach
[2]_____. It is not [3]_____ to be [4]_____ with Alex. He
[5]_____ thinks of things to do and he makes me laugh a lot because he is very
[6]_____.

27

Shopping

I put my shopping in my bag.

I bought a box of chocolates.

I paid by credit card.

I paid cash.

I **went shopping** with my friend Mary. First, we went to a clothes shop. I wanted to **buy** a jacket, but I looked at the **price** and it was too **expensive**. Mary said I should **pay** for it with my **credit card**, but I don't like **spending** money that I don't have.

Good to know!

Make sure you use the correct prepositions. When you use <u>pay</u> with the thing that you buy after it, you must <u>always</u> use <u>for</u>:

I <u>paid for</u> all the food.

You can use <u>by</u> or <u>with a</u> before <u>credit card</u>:

Can I pay <u>by</u> credit card?

She paid <u>with</u> a credit card.

You can use <u>by</u> or <u>with</u> before <u>cash</u>, or you can use <u>cash</u> on its own:

We have to pay <u>by cash</u>.

I paid for the drinks with <u>cash</u>.

He paid <u>cash</u> for the car.

Words for talking about shopping

bag	NOUN A **bag** is a container made of paper, plastic, or leather, used for carrying things.
box	NOUN A **box** is a container with a hard bottom, hard sides, and usually a lid.
buy	VERB If you **buy** something, you get it by paying money for it.
cash	NOUN **Cash** is money in the form of notes and coins.
cheap	ADJECTIVE Things that are **cheap** cost little money.
closed	ADJECTIVE When a shop is **closed**, it is not open and you cannot buy things there.
cost	VERB If something **costs** an amount of money, you have to pay that amount in order to buy it.
credit card	NOUN A **credit card** is a card that you use to buy something and pay for it later.
dollar	NOUN The **dollar** is the unit of money used in the US, Canada, Australia and some other countries.
expensive	ADJECTIVE Things that are **expensive** cost a lot of money.
get	VERB If you **get** something, you buy it.
go shopping	PHRASE If you go to the shops to buy things, you **go shopping**.
open	ADJECTIVE When a shop is **open**, you can go in it and buy things.
pay	VERB When you **pay** for something, you give someone an amount of money for it.
price	NOUN The **price** of something is the amount of money that you have to pay in order to buy it.
sell	VERB If you **sell** something that you own, you let someone have it in return for money.
shop	NOUN A **shop** is a building where people sell things.
shopping	NOUN Your **shopping** is the things you buy from shops.
shut	ADJECTIVE When a shop is **shut**, it is not open and you cannot buy things there.
spend	VERB When you **spend** money, you pay money for things that you want or need.
supermarket	NOUN A **supermarket** is a large shop that sells all kinds of food and other products for the home.

Exercise 1

Put the correct word in each gap.

shut | dollars | bought | spent | went | expensive

Molly and I had a nice morning. We ^{1}_____ shopping and ^{2}_____ a lot

of money. I ^{3}_____ some shoes and a new coat. The coat was ^{4}_____

(a hundred and fifty ^{5}_____!) but it's *really* nice. Molly wanted to go to Green Stores

but it was ^{6}_____. I thought it was open on Sundays but I was wrong.

Exercise 2

Match the sentence halves.

1 While you're at the supermarket,   **a** these bags, please?

2 I bought two pairs of shoes   **b** could you get some butter, please?

3 Could you carry   **c** credit card?

4 A hotel room costs about   **d** because they were so cheap.

5 Can I pay by   **e** 80 dollars a night.

6 I don't know the price   **f** of a litre of milk.

Exercise 3

Complete the sentences by writing one word in each gap.

box | sell | closed | get | paid | shop

1 I've just bought a radio. I haven't taken it out of its _____ yet.

2 I went to the _____ to get some bread and milk.

3 I got to the bank too late and it was _____.

4 Excuse me, do you _____ toothbrushes in this supermarket, please?

5 My dad _____ for the meal. That was nice.

6 If you're going shopping, could you _____ some pasta, please?

Exercise 4

Write the simple past form of the verb in (brackets) to complete each sentence.

1 Hannah and I _____ (go) shopping yesterday.

2 We _____ (buy) a new TV.

3 I _____ (pay) for the food with cash.

4 I _____ (get) a new mobile phone at the weekend.

5 Guy _____ (spend) 300 dollars on a new jacket.

6 My bike was too small for me so I _____ (sell) it to a friend.

Exercise 5

For each question, tick the correct answer.

1 If a shop is *not* shut, it is
☐ closed.
☐ open.

2 Another word for 'buy' is
☐ sell.
☐ get.

3 If something costs only a little money, it is
☐ cheap.
☐ expensive.

4 Metal and paper money is
☐ cash.
☐ price.

5 When you go shopping, you
☐ spend money.
☐ sell money.

Exercise 6

Decide if the pairs of sentences have the same meaning.

1 A The price of food is so high.
  B Food is so expensive. ☐

2 A I bought some new clothes.
  B I got some new clothes. ☐

3 A The shop was shut. ☐
  B The shop was open.

4 A Their clothes are very cheap.
  B Their clothes cost a lot. ☐

5 A Jack paid for the drinks. ☐
  B Jack bought the drinks.

28

Feelings

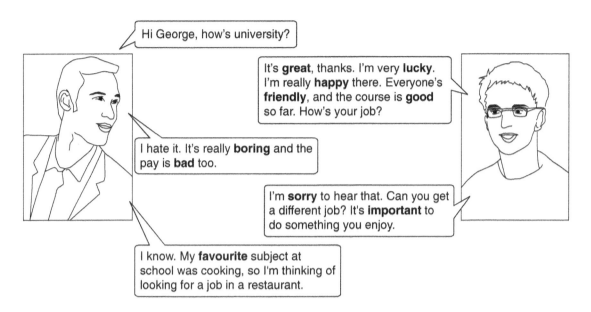

Hi George, how's university?

It's **great**, thanks. I'm very **lucky**. I'm really **happy** there. Everyone's **friendly**, and the course is **good** so far. How's your job?

I hate it. It's really **boring** and the pay is **bad** too.

I'm **sorry** to hear that. Can you get a different job? It's **important** to do something you enjoy.

I know. My **favourite** subject at school was cooking, so I'm thinking of looking for a job in a restaurant.

To: Lily Jones

From: Emma Moore

Subject: France

Hi Lily

Your sister told me you are going to live in Paris for a year, so I wanted to tell you that you must visit my friends, Pierre and Anne. They're so **friendly**, and I know they would love to meet you.

Pierre is a **great** cook – if you make friends with him, you won't be **hungry**! And Anne is really **nice**. She works in a school and she always has lots of **funny** stories about the children there.

Also, be sure to visit the Rodin Museum – it's my **favourite** museum in the world!

I hope you'll be really **happy** in Paris, and I'd love to visit you some time!

Love
Emma
x

Words for talking about feelings

bad	1 ADJECTIVE Something that is **bad** is unpleasant or harmful. 2 ADJECTIVE Something that is **bad** is of a very low standard, quality, or amount.
boring	ADJECTIVE Someone or something that is **boring** is not at all interesting.
favourite	ADJECTIVE **Favourite** is used for describing the thing or person that you like more than all the others.
feelings	PLURAL NOUN Your **feelings** about something are the things you think and feel about it.
fine	ADJECTIVE If you are **fine**, you are well or happy.
friendly	ADJECTIVE If someone is **friendly**, they behave in a pleasant, kind way.
funny	ADJECTIVE Someone or something that is **funny** is amusing and likely to make you smile or laugh.
good	ADJECTIVE **Good** means pleasant or enjoyable.
great	ADJECTIVE If something is **great**, it is very good or enjoyable.
happy	ADJECTIVE Someone who is **happy** feels pleased and satisfied.
hungry	ADJECTIVE When you are **hungry**, you want to eat.
important	ADJECTIVE If something is **important** to you, you feel that you must do, have, or think about it.
lucky	ADJECTIVE You say that someone is **lucky** when they have good luck.
nice	ADJECTIVE If something is **nice**, it is attractive, pleasant, or enjoyable.
sad	ADJECTIVE If you are **sad**, you feel unhappy.
sorry	ADJECTIVE If you are **sorry** about a situation, you feel regret, sadness, or disappointment about it.
tired	ADJECTIVE If you are **tired**, you feel that you want to rest or sleep.

Word Finder

Exercise 1

Choose the correct word.

1 I'm **hungry / great / favourite**. Let's have a pizza.

2 I'm **important / tired / sorry** I'm late. My train stopped for nearly an hour.

3 Caroline didn't enjoy the film. She thought it was very **bad / happy / friendly**.

4 You're **good / lucky / nice** to have a job you enjoy.

5 People laughed a lot at the comedy programme. It was very **boring / funny / sad**.

Exercise 2

Choose the correct word.

Dear Mum and Dad,

Staffordshire is a ¹**great / hungry / sad** place for our holiday. The people are ²**sorry / important / friendly**, the hills are very ³**nice / tired / happy** and we're ⁴**boring / lucky / good** – it's sunny every day. Our ⁵**favourite / funny / bad** place is Consall Hall Gardens. They're beautiful!

See you when we get home.

Love

Lucy and Ewan

Exercise 3

Are the highlighted words correct or incorrect in the sentences?

1 It's **great** ❑ that you can come and stay with me next weekend.

2 Joanna played tennis all afternoon and then she felt very **tired** ❑.

3 I enjoyed the book very much. It was very **boring** ❑.

4 My family is a very **important** ❑ part of my life.

4 Linda is **fine** ❑ and sends you her love.

6 When I had a problem, my friends were very **favourite** ❑ and helped me a lot.

Exercise 4

Complete the sentences by writing one word in each gap.

| tired | hungry | happy | sad | important | funny |

1 It was a very _____ story and I cried when I read it.

2 Trevor slept for 12 hours because he was very _____.

3 If you want to go to university, it's _____ to work hard.

4 I'm _____ to help you, if I can.

5 Sheila had a big lunch, so she doesn't feel _____.

6 I saw a very _____ play at the theatre yesterday. Everyone laughed a lot.

Exercise 5

Which sentences are correct?

1 The weather was sad, so Karl stayed indoors. ❑

2 When Barry went to work in Italy, he was happy that he could speak Italian. ❑

3 When Trish came home, her parents had some sorry news for her. ❑

4 I didn't enjoy science lessons at school because they were boring. ❑

5 My favourite colours are green and brown. ❑

6 Jack is going to bed early because he's got some important work to do tomorrow. ❑

Exercise 6

Complete the sentences by writing one word in each gap.

| favourite | boring | friendly | bad | great | lucky |

1 This is a very _____ town. There's nothing to do here.

2 I like jazz, but my _____ type of music is hip-hop.

3 I'm afraid I've got some _____ news for you.

4 I enjoy my work. The people I meet are always very _____.

5 Dominic had a _____ time in Turkey, so he wants to go back there.

6 Ann went out without an umbrella; she was _____ that it didn't rain.

29

Signs and notices

You use the exit to leave a building.

You can't buy things here at the moment.

They mustn't give bread to the ducks.

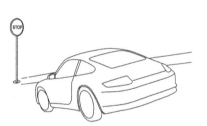

When you see this sign, you must stop.

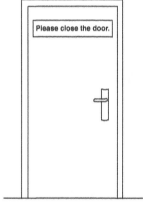

You should not leave the door open.

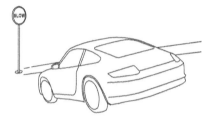

When you see this sign, you must drive slowly.

Good to know!

Remember that _information_ is uncountable. You should never put an 's' at the end of it or 'an' in front of it:

We want _some information_ about train times.

Words for talking about signs and notices

	bus	NOUN A **bus** is a large motor vehicle that carries passengers.
	closed	ADJECTIVE When a shop or place is **closed**, it is not open and you cannot buy or do anything there.
	do not	PHRASE If a sign says **do not** park here, you are not allowed to park your car there.
	exit	NOUN The **exit** is the door that you use to leave a public building.
	gents	NOUN The **gents** is a public toilet for men.
	here	ADVERB You use **here** when you are talking about the place where you are.
	hot	ADJECTIVE Someone or something that is **hot** has a high temperature.
	in	PREPOSITION You use **in** when you are saying where someone or something is.
	information	NOUN **Information** about someone or something is facts about them.
	ladies	NOUN The **ladies** is a public toilet for women.
	lift	NOUN A **lift** is a device that takes people up and down a tall building.
	no parking	PHRASE If a sign says **no parking**, you are not allowed to park your car there.
	no smoking	PHRASE If a sign says **no smoking**, you are not allowed to smoke there.
	notice	NOUN A **notice** is a written announcement in a place where everyone can read it.
	open	ADJECTIVE When a shop or place is **open**, people can go into it.
	out	ADVERB If you go **out** of a place, you leave it.
	sign	NOUN A **sign** is a piece of wood, metal or plastic with words or pictures on it, giving information.
	slow	ADJECTIVE If something is **slow**, it does not move or happen quickly.
	stop	VERB When a moving person or vehicle **stops**, they do not move anymore.
	telephone	NOUN A **telephone** is the piece of equipment that you use for speaking to someone who is in another place.
	toilet	NOUN A **toilet** is a large bowl with a seat that you use when you want to get rid of waste from your body.

Word Finder

Exercise 1

Put each sentence into the correct order.

1 telephone / the / use / speak to / to / your / friends / .

_____

2 not / do / in / go / exit / the / .

_____

3 ladies / toilets / there / are / any / ?

_____

4 no / smoking in / there / is / school / the / .

_____

5 hot in / it / is / here / .

_____

6 can / go / lift / we / up / the / in / ?

_____

Exercise 2

Match the sentence halves.

1 You can buy things here now because
2 Close the window because
3 Stop your car because
4 You can't go out of the park here because
5 Get answers to your questions here because
6 Do not get in the lift because

a it's cold in here.
b it's the information desk.
c the light is red.
d it isn't the exit.
e the shop is open.
f it isn't working.

Exercise 3

Choose the correct word or words.

1 Go **out / in** through the exit.
2 To go into town, go **on the bus / in the lift**.
3 The supermarket is **open / closed** 24 hours a day.
4 To find a hotel, ask someone at **the telephone box / the information desk**.
5 **No parking / No smoking** means you must not put your car here.
6 The gents **toilet / ladies** is here.

Exercise 4

Rearrange the letters to find words. Use the definitions to help you.

1 dilaes _____ (toilet for women and girls)
2 socled _____ (not open)
3 xite _____ (go out this way)
4 frintomanio _____ (ask for this if you don't know it)
5 wols _____ (not fast)
6 plonethee _____ (speak to other people on this)

Exercise 5

Put the correct word in each gap.

| exit | Smoking | bus | gents | in | open | here | lift |

1 toilet _____
2 way of travelling on a road _____
3 way out _____
4 way of going up in a building _____
5 Don't do it. No _____
6 not closed _____

30

Countries, nationalities and languages

Country	Adjective	Language
America	American	English
Australia	Australian	English
USA	American	English
Brazil	Brazilian	Main language: Portuguese
Canada	Canadian	English and French
China	Chinese	Chinese
England	English	English
India	Indian	Many languages spoken.
Italy	Italian	Italian
Russia	Russian	Russian
Spain	Spanish	Spanish

Good to know!

You should only say <u>England</u> when you mean just England, and not Wales, Scotland or Ireland. To talk about all of these countries, use <u>Britain</u>. The adjective is <u>British</u>. The <u>UK</u> means England, Wales, Scotland and Northern Ireland.

Exercise 1

Complete the sentences by writing one word in each gap.

1 Lara works in Italy and she speaks very good _____.

2 My sister married a _____ student she met at university and now she lives in Spain.

3 Many people in India speak excellent _____, but they never visit England.

4 I want to study _____, because my company is doing business with China.

5 I'd like to go to Russia to learn to speak _____ really well.

6 I went to Brazil to meet my _____ cousins.

Exercise 2

Find the words that do not belong, as shown.

1 **Languages**	(Brazilian)	English	Italian
2 **Nationalities**	Canadian	Spanish	England
3 **Countries**	Africa	Spain	China
4 **Continents**	Australia	Africa	USA
5 **Nationalities**	American	Brazilian	India

Exercise 3

Choose the correct word.

1 Does your brother speak **Spain / Spanish** well?

2 My family comes from **Russia / Russian**.

3 What language do people speak in **Brazilian / Brazil**?

4 Do you like **China / Chinese** food?

5 The new **American / USA** film is making millions of dollars.

6 I bought this bag in an **Italy / Italian** shop last week.

Exercise 4

Rearrange the letters to find words. Use the definitions to help you.

1 fArcia _____ (the continent Nelson Mandela comes from)

2 tylla _____ (a great place for pizza and pasta)

3 andli _____ (a hot country with very many languages)

4 liatrasuA _____ (an island and a continent)

5 larBiz _____ (a South American country)

6 sauRis _____ (a country with very cold winters)

Exercise 5

Write one missing word in sentence B so that it means the same as sentence A.

1 A Luca is Italian.

   B Luca comes from _____.

2 A Isabella is from Spain.

   B Isabella is _____.

3 A I have several Chinese friends.

   B I have several friends from _____.

4 A My favourite band is from the USA.

   B My favourite band is _____.

5 A There are some beautiful lakes in Canada.

   B The _____ lakes are beautiful.

Exercise 6

Match the places with the maps.

1 Australia   **a**

2 Africa   **b**

3 Canada   **c**

4 Russia   **d**

5 Brazil   **e**

6 Spain   **f**

Answer key

1 Talking about yourself

Exercise 1

1 first
2 family
3 lives
4 years
5 student
6 college

Exercise 2

1 c
2 a
3 e
4 d
5 b
6 f

Exercise 3

1 city
2 Peter
3 family
4 job
5 years old

Exercise 4

1 name
2 work
3 family
4 university
5 study
6 born

Exercise 5

1 it
2 address
3 age
4 country
5 school
6 work

2 Family

Exercise 1

1 boy
2 family
3 grandfather
4 young
5 old
6 daughter
7 family name
8 old

Exercise 2

1 years old
2 brother
3 young
4 mum
5 children
6 family

Exercise 3

1 Yes
2 No
3 No
4 Yes
5 No
6 Yes

Exercise 4

1 the
2 name
3 brother
4 girls
5 much
6 old

Exercise 5

1 family name ✗
2 young ✓
3 children ✓
4 mother ✗
5 dads ✗
6 grandma ✗

3 House and home

Exercise 1

1 lives
2 bedroom
3 living room
4 kitchen
5 dining room
6 windows

Exercise 2

1 b
2 f
3 d
4 a
5 e
6 c

Exercise 3

1 address
2 garden
3 wall
4 bedrooms
5 chair
6 window

Exercise 4

1 some chairs.
2 door.
3 flat.
4 walls.
5 kitchen.
6 bathroom.

Exercise 5

1 b
2 f
3 c
4 d
5 e
6 a

Exercise 6

1 window
2 toilet
3 garden
4 dining room
5 address
6 flat

4 Describing objects

Exercise 1

1 glass
2 red
3 under
4 below
5 big
6 bottom
7 paper
8 behind

Exercise 2

1	blue	4	below your head
2	glass	5	outside a house
3	paper		

Exercise 3

1	different	4	outside
2	big	5	bottom
3	glass	6	important

Exercise 4

1	outside	4	bottom
2	paper	5	important
3	under	6	inside

Exercise 5

1	above	3	at
2	behind	4	inside

Exercise 6

1	Yes	4	Yes
2	Yes	5	No
3	No	6	Yes

5 Parts of the body and describing people

Exercise 1

1	mouth	4	nose
2	feet	5	hands
3	ears	6	skin

Exercise 2

1	No	4	Yes
2	Yes	5	No
3	No	6	Yes

Exercise 3

1	hair	4	foot *or* leg
2	beard	5	eyes
3	body	6	hand

Exercise 4

1	bald ✓	4	teeth ✓
2	legs ✓	5	arms ✗
3	hands ✗	6	eyes ✓

6 Clothes

Exercise 1

1	Clothes.	4	Shorts.
2	In cold weather.	5	When you play tennis.
3	On my arm.	6	A shirt.

Exercise 2

1	d	4	e
2	a	5	b
3	f	6	c

Exercise 3

1	jeans	4	jacket
2	skirt	5	clothes
3	umbrella	6	T-shirt

Exercise 4

1	gloves	4	shorts
2	socks	5	hat
3	umbrella	6	watch

Exercise 5

1	shirt	4	hat
2	shoes	5	sweater
3	gloves	6	jacket

Exercise 6

1 You put on your socks before your shoes.

2 I wear shorts at the beach.

3 Take an umbrella because it's raining.

4 I'm buying my mum a scarf for her birthday.

5 Sam is putting on his coat because it's cold.

6 Pam is wearing her new dress.

7 Talking about people

Exercise 1

1	young.	4	boring.
2	short.	5	happy.
3	small.	6	clever.

Exercise 2

1	e	4	a
2	c	5	b
3	f	6	d

Exercise 3

1	slim	4	beautiful
2	clever	5	boring
3	nice	6	old

Exercise 4

1	young	4	old
2	short	5	clever
3	happy	6	man

Exercise 5

1	adults	4	baby
2	tired	5	young
3	woman	6	girls

Exercise 6

1 d	4 c
2 a	5 e
3 f	6 b

8 School and university

Exercise 1

1 subject	4 board
2 exam	5 school
3 lessons	6 learn

Exercise 2

1 teacher	4 learned
2 lessons	5 read
3 classroom	6 books

Exercise 3

1 b	4 a
2 e	5 d
3 c	6 f

Exercise 4

1 class ✗	4 university ✓
2 dictionary ✓	5 homework ✓
3 school ✗	6 lesson ✗

Exercise 5

1 What is your favourite subject?

2 Ten students took the French course.

3 My brother is studying history at university.

4 Our English teacher doesn't give us much homework.

5 Are we going to have a spelling test?

6 I'd like to learn to sing.

9 Sports and leisure

Exercise 1

1 b	4 a
2 e	5 c
3 d	

Exercise 2

1 tennis	4 football
2 sailing	5 race
3 quiz	6 run

Exercise 3

1 I'd like to go swimming after school.

2 The captain wants the players to win the match.

3 My sister and I had a good game of tennis.

4 My father goes sailing but I prefer playing basketball.

5 There's a good pool at the sports centre.

6 The old men go fishing but the young men play football.

Exercise 4

1 Yes	4 No
2 Yes	5 Yes
3 Yes	6 No

10 Work and jobs

Exercise 1

1 guide	4 job
2 actor	5 businessman
3 company	6 manager

Exercise 2

1 c	4 e
2 a	5 d
3 b	6 f

Exercise 3

1 c	4 e
2 a	5 d
3 f	6 b

Exercise 4

1 teacher	4 singer, actor
2 doctor, nurse	5 farmer
3 pilot	6 photographer

Exercise 5

1 policewoman	4 farmer
2 manager	5 guide
3 teacher	6 photographer

Exercise 6

1 police officers ✓	4 job ✓
2 secretary ✗	5 office ✓
3 worker ✗	6 factory ✗

11 Daily routines

Exercise 1

1 listens	4 goes
2 watches	5 does
3 eats	6 has

Exercise 2

1 drive	4 In the morning
2 get up	5 have
3 have	6 play

Exercise 3

1 to   4 in
2 on   5 Get
3 go   6 a

Exercise 4

1 Yes   4 Yes
2 No   5 No
3 No   6 Yes

Exercise 5

1 up   4 out
2 In   5 eat
3 go   6 watch

12 Words that are used together (collocations)

Exercise 1

1 guitar   4 football
2 breakfast   5 married
3 shower   6 school

Exercise 2

1 a   4 d
2 b   5 c
3 e

Exercise 3

1 school   4 breakfast
2 job   5 shower
3 time   6 piano

Exercise 4

1 got   4 have
2 capital   5 free
3 start   6 mark

Exercise 5

1 Yes   4 Yes
2 No   5 No
3 No   6 Yes

Exercise 6

1 email address   4 phone number
2 play football   5 go home
3 get a job   6 leave school

13 Time

Exercise 1

1 e   4 c
2 f   5 d
3 a   6 b

Exercise 2

1 Why are you late?
2 My birthday is on Wednesday.
3 What time are you going to work today?
4 Our English class is at six fifteen.
5 Are you free on Sunday?
6 Would you like to come to my party?

Exercise 3

1 evening   4 thirty
2 late   5 It's 16.20.
3 eleven   6 five thirty

Exercise 4

1 the   4 for
2 on   5 to
3 on   6 it

Exercise 5

1 ninety   4 eight thirty
2 forty-five 5 seven
3 twelve twenty   6 twenty

14 Transport

Exercise 1

1 d   4 f
2 c   5 a
3 e   6 b

Exercise 2

1 f   4 a
2 c   5 b
3 d   6 e

Exercise 3

1 a plane   4 a bicycle
2 a coach   5 a car
3 a taxi   6 a station

Exercise 4

1 trip   4 far
2 coach   5 car
3 taxi   6 near

Exercise 5

1 train   4 ticket
2 plane   5 road
3 coach   6 bicycle

Exercise 6

1 ticket ✓   4 coatch ✗
2 naer ✗   5 trip ✓
3 stasion ✗   6 trane ✗

15 In town

Exercise 1

1 b   4 d
2 f   5 a
3 c   6 e

Exercise 2

1 airport   4 road
2 café   5 market
3 bank   6 school

Exercise 3

1 restaurant   4 hotel
2 library   5 car park
3 bus stop   6 road

Exercise 4

1 flat   4 street
2 hotels   5 café
3 station   6 cinema

Exercise 5

1 b   4 d
2 a   5 c
3 e   6 f

Exercise 6

1 We often walk in the park.
2 Jill buys food at the market.
3 The museum has lots of old things.
4 Tom's school is in this street.
5 That café sells good coffee.
6 You can see our road on this map.

16 Health, medicine and exercise

Exercise 1

1 exercise   4 body
2 hospital   5 nurse
3 babies   6 hear

Exercise 2

1 f   4 d
2 e   5 b
3 c   6 a

Exercise 3

1 headache.   4 neck.
2 a cold.   5 sick.
3 problem.   6 exercise.

Exercise 4

1 d   4 f
2 e   5 c
3 b   6 a

Exercise 5

1 cough   4 problem
2 baby   5 hear
3 exercise   6 hospital

Exercise 6

1 doctor, nurse   4 sick, tired
2 hospital   5 exercise
3 neck   6 toothache

17 Food

Exercise 1

1 f   4 e
2 a   5 c
3 d   6 b

Exercise 2

1 lunch   4 butter
2 coffee   5 vegetables
3 apples   6 chocolate

Exercise 3

1 d   4 f
2 e   5 a
3 b   6 c

Exercise 4

1 We usually have rice and vegetables for dinner.
2 I took some bread and cheese for my lunch.
3 You can buy good fruit and vegetables at the market.
4 I often eat chocolate after dinner.
5 I had a plate of chips with my salad.
6 I always have coffee with my breakfast.

Exercise 5

1 some cheese   4 a banana
2 meat   5 fish
3 a cake   6 fruit

Exercise 6

1 fruit   4 milk
2 eats   5 cake
3 lunch   6 drinks

18 Talking about what you like

Exercise 1

1 c
4 e
2 b
5 a
3 d

Exercise 2

1 like
4 fun
2 prefer
5 enjoy
3 want
6 hope

Exercise 3

1 No
4 Yes
2 Yes
5 No
3 Yes
6 No

Exercise 4

1 interesting ✓
4 like ✗
2 thirsty ✓
5 good ✓
3 love ✗
6 enjoy ✗

Exercise 5

1 f
4 e
2 a
5 d
3 c
6 b

Exercise 6

1 thirsty
4 great
2 interesting
5 hungry
3 lovely
6 tired

19 Travel and holidays

Exercise 1

1 visit
4 ticket
2 hotels
5 taxi
3 travel
6 leaves

Exercise 2

1 by ✓
4 Go ✗
2 get ✗
5 get ✓
3 driver ✓
6 visit ✗

Exercise 3

1 by
4 station
2 to
5 visited
3 drives
6 ticket

Exercise 4

1 travel
4 get
2 by
5 visit
3 leave
6 boat

Exercise 5

1 No
4 Yes
2 Yes
5 No
3 No
6 No

20 Weather

Exercise 1

1 Yes
4 No
2 Yes
5 No
3 No
6 Yes

Exercise 2

1 f
4 c
2 b
5 a
3 d
6 e

Exercise 3

1 snow
4 rains
2 sky
5 summer
3 cloudy
6 sunny

Exercise 4

1 ice
4 cloud
2 foggy
5 summer
3 windy
6 snow

Exercise 5

1 cloud ✓
4 fog ✗
2 sun ✗
5 hot ✓
3 wind ✗
6 raining ✓

Exercise 6

1 cloud
4 winter
2 wet
5 sunny
3 weather
6 fog

21 Natural world

Exercise 1

1 beach
4 summer
2 forest
5 weather
3 flower
6 world

Exercise 2

1 f
4 a
2 e
5 d
3 c
6 b

Exercise 3

1 sun
4 grass
2 forest
5 snow
3 tree

Exercise 4

1 sun   4 rains
2 forest   5 weather
3 snow

Exercise 5

1 world ✓   4 warm ✓
2 trees ✗   5 rain ✓
3 weather ✗   6 summer ✗

Exercise 6

1 river   4 sea
2 forest   5 beach
3 tree   6 summer

22 Entertainment and the media

Exercise 1

1 group   4 radio
2 guitar   5 films
3 sang   6 cinemas

Exercise 2

1 b   4 d
2 e   5 a
3 f   6 c

Exercise 3

1 Yes   4 No
2 No   5 Yes
3 No   6 Yes

Exercise 4

1 music ✓   4 band ✗
2 cinemas ✗   5 camera ✓
3 drawing ✓   6 sings ✓

Exercise 5

1 picture   4 band
2 radio   5 photos
3 pages

Exercise 6

1 b   4 e
2 c   5 f
3 a   6 d

23 Phrases with do, get, go, have, make and take

Exercise 1

1 c   4 b
2 d   5 a
3 f   6 e

Exercise 2

1 had   4 gets
2 had   5 do
3 get   6 got

Exercise 3

1 My father has blue eyes.
2 I have a really bad cold.
3 Could you get some bread, please?
4 We had some delicious food.
5 I got a bus to the restaurant.
6 I took my phone with me.

Exercise 4

1 made   4 took
2 got   5 had
3 went   6 did

Exercise 5

1 d   4 c
2 b   5 f
3 e   6 a

24 Words that connect sentences

Exercise 1

1 e   4 a
2 d   5 c
3 b   6 f

Exercise 2

1 when   4 so
2 also   5 but
3 because   6 or

Exercise 3

1 or ✗   4 because ✗
2 and ✓   5 So ✓
3 Now ✓   6 Well ✓

Exercise 4

1 also   4 Well
2 Now   5 So
3 Really   6 OK

Exercise 5

1 Yes   4 No
2 No   5 Yes
3 Yes   6 Yes

Exercise 6

1 Well, I'm very pleased you're here.
2 Now, who wants an ice cream?
3 When shall we go home?
4 OK, you can swim in the river.

5 Really? I didn't know that!

6 So where do you come from?

25 Where things are

Exercise 1
1 No

2 No

3 Yes

4 Yes

5 No

6 Yes

Exercise 2
1 address

2 outside

3 top

4 below

5 by

Exercise 3
1 at

2 map

3 place

4 near

5 out of

6 opposite

Exercise 4
1 I went downstairs to get my watch.

2 Andy took his key out of his pocket.

3 We walked to the top of the hill.

4 The footballer sat below a photo of the sports centre.

5 I can only use my phone outside the house.

6 Kirsten has lunch at a café opposite her office.

Exercise 5
1 outside

2 before

3 bottom

4 address

5 opposite

6 downstairs

26 What is it like? How is it done?

Exercise 1
1 funny.

2 bored.

3 clean.

4 difficult.

5 possible.

6 careful.

Exercise 2
1 e

2 b

3 d

4 c

5 a

6 f

Exercise 3
1 correct

2 fast

3 quick

4 last

5 difficult

6 clean

Exercise 4
1 My sister never reads books.

2 Ivan's English is very poor.

3 Anna plays the piano very well.

4 We always walk to school together.

5 This is a very slow train.

6 Is it OK to take this chair?

Exercise 5
1 clean

2 good

3 slow

4 last

5 difficult

6 early

Exercise 6
1 good

2 together

3 possible

4 bored

5 always

6 funny

27 Shopping

Exercise 1
1 went

2 spent

3 bought

4 expensive

5 dollars

6 shut

Exercise 2
1 b

2 d

3 a

4 e

5 c

6 f

Exercise 3
1 box

2 shop

3 closed

4 sell

5 paid

6 get

Exercise 4
1 went

2 bought

3 paid

4 got

5 spent

6 sold

Exercise 5
1 open.

2 get.

3 cheap.

4 cash.

5 spend money.

Exercise 6
1 Yes

2 Yes

3 No

4 No

5 Yes

28 Feelings

Exercise 1

1 hungry
2 sorry
3 bad
4 lucky
5 funny

Exercise 2

1 great
2 friendly
3 nice
4 lucky
5 favourite

Exercise 3

1 great ✓
2 tired ✓
3 boring ✗
4 important ✓
5 fine ✓
6 favourite ✗

Exercise 4

1 sad
2 tired
3 important
4 happy
5 hungry
6 funny

Exercise 5

1 No
2 Yes
3 No
4 Yes
5 Yes
6 Yes

Exercise 6

1 boring
2 favourite
3 bad
4 friendly
5 great
6 lucky

29 Signs and notices

Exercise 1

1 Use the telephone to speak to your friends.
2 Do not go in the exit.
3 Are there any ladies toilets?
4 There is no smoking in the school.
5 It is hot in here.
6 Can we go up in the lift?

Exercise 2

1 e
2 a
3 c
4 d
5 b
6 f

Exercise 3

1 out
2 on the bus
3 open
4 the information desk
5 No parking
6 toilet

Exercise 4

1 ladies
2 closed
3 exit
4 information
5 slow
6 telephone

Exercise 5

1 gents
2 bus
3 exit
4 lift
5 Smoking
6 open

30 Countries, nationalities and languages

Exercise 1

1 Italian
2 Spanish
3 English
4 Chinese
5 Russian
6 Brazilian

Exercise 2

1 Brazilian
2 England
3 Africa
4 USA
5 India

Exercise 3

1 Spanish
2 Russia
3 Brazil
4 Chinese
5 American
6 Italian

Exercise 4

1 Africa
2 Italy
3 India
4 Australia
5 Brazil
6 Russia

Exercise 5

1 Italy
2 Spanish
3 China
4 American
5 Canadian

Exercise 6

1 d
2 f
3 e
4 a
5 b
6 c

Index

The numbers refer to the unit numbers, not page numbers.

E

ear 5
earache 16
early 26
eat 17
egg 17
email address 12
enjoy 18
entertainment 22
evening 13
exam 8
exercise 16
exit 29
expensive 27
eye 5

F

face 5
factory 10
family 1, 2
family name 1, 2
far 14
farmer 10
fast 26
fast food 12
father 2
favourite 28
feelings 28
film 22
fine 28
first 26
first name 1
fish 17
fishing 9
flat 3, 15
flower 21
fly 19
fog 20
foggy 20
food 17
football 9
forest 21
free time 12
friendly 28
fruit 17
full stop 12
fun 18
funny 26, 28

G

game 9
garden 3
gents 29

get 27
get married 12
girl 2, 7
glass 4
glove 6
go 14, 25
good 18, 26, 28
go shopping 27
go to work 12
grandad 2
grandfather 2
grandma 2
grandmother 2
grass 21
great 18, 28
green 4
group 22
guide 10
guitar 22

H

hair 5
half past 13
happy 7, 18, 28
hat 6
head 5
headache 16
health 16
hear 16
here 29
holiday 19
home 3
homework 8
hope 18
hospital 16
hot 18, 20, 21, 29
hotel 15, 19
house 3
hungry 18, 28
hurt 16

I

ice 20
important 4, 28
in 29
information 29
inside 4
interesting 18

J

jacket 6
jeans 6
job 1, 10

K

key 3
kitchen 3

L

ladies 29
last 26
late 13
learn 8
leave 19
leg 5, 16
leisure 9
lesson 8
letter 12
library 15
lift 29
like 18
little 7
live 1, 3
living room 3
love 18
lovely 18
lucky 28
lunch 17

M

man 2, 7
manager 10
map 15, 25
mark 12
market 15
married 12
match 9
meat 17
media 22
medicine 16
milk 17
minute 13
Monday 13
morning 13
mother 2
movie 22
mum 2
museum 15
music 22

N

name 1, 2
nationality 1
near 14, 25
neck 16
never 26
newspaper 22

U

umbrella 6
under 4
university 1, 8
up 25

V

vegetables 17
visit 19

W

wall 3
want 18
warm 20, 21
watch 6
wear 6
weather 20, 21
Wednesday 13
week 13
well 24, 26
wet 20
when 24
white 4
wind 20
window 3
windy 20
winter 20, 21
woman 7
work 1, 10, 12
worker 10
world 21
would like 18

Y

yellow 4
young 2, 7

Collins

Work on your Grammar
Over 200 exercises to improve your English grammar

A1 Elementary
978-0-00-749953-3

A2 Pre-intermediate
978-0-00-749954-0

B1 Intermediate
978-0-00-749962-5

B2 Upper Intermediate
978-0-00-749963-2

C1 Advanced
978-0-00-749967-0

Work on your Vocabulary
Hundreds of words to learn and remember

A1 Elementary
978-0-00-749954-0

A2 Pre-intermediate
978-0-00-749957-1

B1 Intermediate
978-0-00-749964-9

B2 Upper Intermediate
978-0-00-749965-6

C1 Advanced
978-0-00-749968-7

collins.co.uk/elt